A NURTURING BLIGHT

*How the One-Room School Experience
Can Inform Modern Educators*

Susan M. Leist

University Press of America,® Inc.
Lanham · Boulder · New York · Toronto · Plymouth, UK

Copyright © 2011 by
University Press of America,® Inc.
4501 Forbes Boulevard
Suite 200
Lanham, Maryland 20706
UPA Acquisitions Department (301) 459-3366

Estover Road
Plymouth PL6 7PY
United Kingdom

Library of Congress Control Number: 2011920128
ISBN: 978-0-7618-5473-9 (paperback : alk. paper)

Table of Contents

Preface

Publishing this book has made this author one of the most surprised people in academia. When I conducted this study as my dissertation in 1989-1990, I had some thought of publishing it—someday. I was, however, a single parent with three children. Two of those children had been in college during the two full-time years I spent at the University of Virginia finishing my doctorate, so we were in danger of starvation if I did not find a job. I came to Buffalo State College in December of 1990 as an assistant professor. Recently, I was awarded the ultimate promotion in the State University of New York system, to SUNY Distinguished Teaching Professor. Although I have published four other books in the course of those twenty years and three promotions, the day just never came that I had time to get back to my dissertation.

My colleague, Dr. Paul Theobald, deserves the credit for making me seek a publisher for this work. An expert in rural education, Paul came to Buffalo State as the first holder of the Woods-Beal Endowed Chair in Urban and Rural Education. He read this study, and he told me that he thought it was an important document to share with the world. His reasons were that the locale of the study was Buckingham County, Virginia, the county adjacent to Prince Edward County, Virginia.

Prince Edward County is an infamous locale in the history of American education for this reason. When the United States Supreme Court ordered the schools of America to be integrated as a result of the *Brown vs. Board of Education* lawsuits, Prince Edward County shut down their public schools rather than comply. Those schools remained closed until 1964. White students in the county were served by the Prince Edward Academy, but black students were not served at all. As a result, the counties like Buckingham surrounding Prince Edward kept their one-room schools open until 1966 in order to serve the black students from Prince Edward County. The Virginia Historical Society's online exhibition on the Civil Rights Movement in Virginia tells the story:

After Virginia's school-closing law was ruled unconstitutional in January 1959, the General Assembly repealed the compulsory school attendance law and made the operation of public schools a local option for the state's counties and cities. Schools that had been closed in Front Royal, Norfolk, and Charlottesville reopened because citizens there preferred integrated schools to none at all. It was not so Prince Edward County. Ordered on May 1, 1959, to integrate its schools, the county instead closed its entire public school system.

The Prince Edward Foundation created a series of private schools to educate the county's white children. These schools were supported by tuition grants from the state and tax credits from the county. Prince Edward Academy became the prototype for all-white private schools formed to protest school integration.

No provision was made for educating the county's black children. Some got schooling with relatives in nearby communities or at makeshift schools in church basements. Others were educated out of state by groups such as the Society of Friends. In 1963–64, the Prince Edward Free School picked up some of the slack. But some pupils missed part or all of their education for five years.

Edward R. Murrow, the famous radio and television journalist, presented the program *The Lost Class of '59* on the CBS television network. It caused national indignation. Nonetheless, not until 1964, when the U.S. Supreme Court outlawed Virginia's tuition grants to private education, did Prince Edward County reopen its schools, on an integrated basis. This event marked the real end of "massive resistance."[1]

Two of the teacher/student respondents in my study were Mr. Frank Harris, the African-American administrator, and Dr. James Anderson, the white administrator. These gentlemen were the first administrators in the newly integrated Buckingham County School district. Dr. Anderson was the Superintendent of Schools, and Mr. Harris was the Assistant Superintendent of Schools. In Chapter Four, the two were members of the group of four respondents who came together in a "A Gathering of Teachers." It was obvious that the two were old and respected enemies.

This study was a fascinating experience for me. In 2010, the publication year for this book, many of the voices recorded here have been stilled, but what they had to say in evoking their experience in the one-room schools, both black and white is still as compelling and true as it was then. My research question, "How can the experiences of people who taught in or went to one-room, one-teacher schools in a rural Virginia county inform the practice of modern educators?" produced answers that I have recorded in Chapter Five and that seem to be even more valid now than they were at the time. Perhaps their publication may plant some seeds in the consciousness of the readers of this book that will bear fruit. I hope so.

Notes

1. "Civil Rights." http://www.vahistorical.org/civilrights/pec.html.

Chapter One
An Introduction

This study is a naturalistic inquiry of selected one-room schools that existed in Buckingham County during the decades after 1910. I chose that time frame because my primary strategy of inquiry was the interview, and the respondents who were available had experiences within that time frame. The question that this study addresses is: How can the experiences of people who taught in or went to one-room, one-teacher schools in a rural Virginia county inform the practice of modern educators? To address this question, I delineated defining characteristics of these schools and discussed the implications of their reinvention in modern schooling.

My interest as a researcher in the one-room school situation came out of a project done for a qualitative research methods course at the University of Virginia's Curry School in the spring of 1989. For that project, I interviewed at length five people who were involved in the one-room schools that had existed at Wingina, Virginia in the 1920's and 1930's. Three of these were students who attended the schools, and two were teachers who taught in them. The data contained in those interviews described an educational experience which had fostered personal growth for both students and teachers of a kind that may have been left behind in the evolution of today's schools. My experience of modern schooling both as a teacher and a parent suggested to me that there was something to be learned from one-room, one-teacher schooling.

The ownership of learning that these five respondents experienced in the one-room school was notable. Their sense of learning and personal growth was to them the most important part of schooling. They also expressed the feeling that the schools belonged to the community in many ways: the buildings had been built by community members, the teachers hired at the request of and with the approval of community representatives, and the curricula determined with input from community members interested in having children prepared for life in the community. The schools functioned as social centers for the community and were a common responsibility among the adult population.

I began to wonder if the respondents' experience of personal growth and ownership were a feature common among others' memories of the one-room schools. Interviewing these participants in one-room schools gave me the impression that the learning environment in their classrooms might be different in some ways from the environment I had experienced as a teacher in a centralized rural system during the years 1980-1988. My experience included many frustrations. For example, I often dealt with parents who regarded the school system as their enemy. Their feeling stemmed from confusion over the grading, discipline, and attendance systems, all based on policies over which they felt they had little or no control. I was unable to mitigate their confusion when the underlying principles of these systems were often in conflict with my own educational philosophy.

My pedagogy was frustrated in various ways. I was required, for example, to teach from the textbooks provided by the school board. These texts frequently were above the reading levels of my students and their contents irrelevant to my students' needs. Also, I felt administrative pressure to assign numerical grades to every paper, however small, produced by students in my classes and to arbitrarily assign homework. Such constraints made record-keeping and compliance with school policies and rules appear to be more highly valued than learning.

In contrast, the one-room school that I had investigated for my 1989 project had learning as the most important consideration within the teacher-student community as well as in the community at large. As indicated above, ownership of learning was a distinguishing feature of the respondent interviews in that study. To examine this and other characteristics of a larger sample of one-room schools, I carried out a series of interviews with people who taught in and/or were students in one-room schools within Buckingham County, Virginia. Among the common characteristics that emerged from the data that were contained in both the original and the larger study are those which appear to have nurtured personal growth, like peer teaching, multi-level classes, and close local control. Additionally, because my major field is English education, I was particularly interested in how reading, writing, speaking, and listening instruction were enacted. The data on that enactment reveals much that is currently considered new in ELA.

I chose Buckingham County for this study for several reasons. Buckingham is a rural county located in the Piedmont area of central Virginia. The county contains the geographical center of the state at Mt. Rush Farm. It is suited to such research because it is a rural county where one-room schools were the major mode of delivery for elementary education through the 1940's, and it was logistically suited to me as a researcher since my home of ten years was located there at the time. As an established member of the community, I started my research from a trust base which I would not have enjoyed elsewhere.

As a former Buckingham County teacher well known to the school board, I had ready access to school board archives. My knowledge as a community member of such data as historical society records provided materials from which I could triangulate and establish trustworthiness in this study. I had access to a variety of materials which reveal the general ambiance of Buckingham County's one-room schools with their instructional and administrative practices, aspects essential to my purpose of discerning how these practices affected students and teachers in the one-room, one-teacher schools.

Historical and Theoretical Origins of This Study

In the 1980's, public education was criticized in the federally sponsored report *A Nation at Risk: The Imperative for Educational Reform*[1] which warned of "a rising tide of mediocrity" in schools. In 1987, former Secretary of Education William Bennett was still publicly criticizing schools, giving them "an overall grade of no better than a 'C' or 'C+'" (Time magazine, Nov. 14, 1988). Currently, in 2010, though much has changed with regard to William Bennett's reputation, little has changed either in Bennett's public criticism or in the mediocre quality of public schooling in America. The year 2002 saw the enactment of *The No Child Left Behind Act of 2001*[2] often abbreviated in print as NCLB and sometimes shortened in pronunciation to "nicklebee,"[3] is a United States Act of Congress that was originally proposed by the administration of President George W. Bush immediately after taking office. The bill, shepherded through the Senate by Senator Ted Kennedy, one of the bill's sponsors, received overwhelming bipartisan support in Congress.[4] President Bush signed it into law on January 8, 2002. NCLB is the latest federal legislation that enacts the theories of standards-based education reform which is based on the belief that setting high standards and establishing measurable goals can improve individual outcomes in education. The Act requires states to develop assessments in basic skills to be given to all students in certain grades, if those states are to receive federal funding for schools. The Act does not assert a national achievement standard; standards are set by each individual state. Since enactment, Congress increased federal funding of education, from $42.2 billion in 2001 to $54.4 billion in 2007.

No Child Left Behind received a 40.4% increase from $17.4 billion in 2001 to $24.4 billion. The funding for reading quadrupled from $286 million in 2001 to $1.2 billion. At the beginning, it seemed that NCLB was going to exert and achieve long awaited reform. In 2005, former Assistant Secretary of Education Diane Ravitch wrote, "We should thank President George W. Bush and Congress for passing the No Child Left Behind Act. . . . All this attention and focus is paying off for younger students, who are reading and solving mathematics problems better than their parents' generation."[5]

One of the problems with the bill, though, was the narrowness of the focus to reading and mathematics. Four years later, Ravitch has changed her mind. "I was known as a conservative advocate of many of these policies," Ravitch says. "But I've looked at the evidence and I've concluded they're wrong. They've put us on the wrong track. I feel passionately about the improvement of public education and I don't think any of this is going to improve public education."[6]

Numerous critics outside the government as well, Hirsch[7] and Bloom[8] among them, have charged that the public school system is not as effective as it could be. Many newspapers currently feature articles which criticize American education. The most stinging criticisms are often related to the estimated thirty million Americans who are functionally illiterate.[9] Critics like Kozol[10] point to the fact that, by a variety of measures, the American school system is not satisfying American taxpayers, parents, students, administrators, or teachers. SAT scores, comparisons between American and Japanese education, and surveys are examples of the measures employed. Modern educators find themselves facing crises emerging in so many aspects of the system that they appear like little Dutch boys at the dikes, unable to staunch the flood. Commissioned studies like *A Nation at Risk*, documents like Virginia's Standards of Learning and *The No Child left Behind Act of 2001*, and programs like Virginia's "Beginning Teacher Assistance Program" indicate that those who are concerned view public education as something to be "fixed." These studies and programs are attempts to alter or adjust the existing system in order to improve it so that it will be more effective.

An earlier attempt to "fix" education in Virginia had as its target a major method of delivering education early in the 20th century, the one-room school. According to Mark Dewalt,[11] there were only 674 public one-room schools operating in the United States in 1987. Only five of those were in the South. Most of the public one-room schools operating then were in the western United States where the low population density made the one-room school a logical school organizational pattern. In 2010, there are a very few still operating, six, for example in Huron County, Michigan. Twenty-first century one-room schools are, of course, completely hooked in to the rest of the district electronically.

The elimination of this kind of school in Virginia, as well as in the rest of the South at least, was an early attempt to "fix" education. In his book called *A Hard Country and A Lonely Place*[12] William A. Link has told the story of how that attempt came about in Virginia as well as the rest of the South. Link says that in the last decades of the nineteenth century and the first decade of the twentieth, social reform for the South was a burning issue, an issue engendered by the Civil War. Education came to be seen as a primary instrument of change by social reformers, both those born in the South and those intersectionalists who came down from the North to aid and guide such reform. The South, and Virginia in particular, was viewed by much of the rest of the country and certainly by Northern reformers as being backward, isolated, and assiduously provincial. Its populace was viewed as being undereducated. Since much of Virginia was rural, rural education was a prime target for reform. According to Link, Virginians themselves were "perhaps never happier" with their schools than in the post-Reconstruction era:

There was little evidence of popular discontent with post-Reconstruction education. Schools appeared to fulfill local expectations: they existed only if parents valued education, could afford schools and were willing to support them with adequate enrollments and attendance. By these measures at least, community-controlled education succeeded. The number of schools steadily increased during the last third of the nineteenth century as did enrollments and attendance; an increasing level of literacy among whites and particularly blacks suggests that rural schools served an expected, if limited, function.[13]

However, the "insiders" of the Virginia school system, state officials and urban educators who strongly felt their lack of control over rural schools, wanted and welcomed reform. They welcomed the report of the NEA Committee of Twelve in 1897. Written by state officials and urban educators of the rural middle west, it was a blueprint for reform which proposed a complete transformation of the "structure, pedagogy, and purposes of rural education."[14] Edwin Christian Glass and other Virginia urban educators responded very positively to the document and used it as a model to articulate reform plans. These plans, however, had very little effect on the school system until reformers outside the school system contributed help and support in the form of influence, financing, and publicity.

These reformers from outside the school system were made up of several groups. Of these, Link first mentions the Richmond civic groups dominated by middle-class but wealthy and socially ambitious women. An example of a reform oriented group formed by such women is the Richmond Education Association which was later subsumed by the Co-operative Education Association since the REA could not produce the male leadership felt necessary for the group to be effective.[15] Another component of the reformers were philanthropists—Northern and Southern—led by such people as Robert Curtis Ogden, a partner of John B. Wanamaker and an evangelical Presbyterian who later succeeded in interesting John D. Rockefeller in the cause of Southern reform and educational reform. These men, in co-operation later with such Southern intersectionalists as Jabez Lamar Monroe Curry and Edwin Anderson Alderman, supported the reform movement for rural education in Virginia and planted the seeds of its success.[16] (These diverse people were united by several beliefs, all of which may be summarized in this statement:

> Intersectionalists concluded that systemic change depended on institutional change, which in turn depended on transforming public education. . . . All were also in general agreement on the deficiencies of rural schools and the changes that would properly remedy them. They agreed that the country schools posed the most serious obstacles to reform.[17]

The first two decades of the twentieth century were spent by these reform groups and their actual agents in trying to transform public education. They made a great amount of progress during those years with the rural school systems. The University of Virginia became a center for teacher training, curriculum development, high school accreditation, and inspection. Many women had entered the profession, and there were normal schools for training these female teachers at Farmville, Radford, Harrisonburg, and Fredericksburg. Link, though, makes this comment about the slowness of the reformers' progress in overcoming the serious obstacle of the country school:

> Side by side with the emerging modernized school system, however, were inescapable vestiges of the past. Although considerable headway was made in reducing the number of small schools, as late as 1920, one-room schools constituted a third of all school-rooms in the state.[18]

The activities of the reformers against the one-room schools had to be intensified through influence from the state governmental level:

> A more visible symbol of the old country school, the dilapidated one-room school, became an object of further change, as state officials used compulsion and incentives to stimulate the construction of permanent modern facilities in secondary schools and consolidated elementary schools.[19]

From all that William Link says about the reform effort in Virginia and the rest of the South, it is clear that the one-teacher, one-room schools had to be altered before intersectionalists could use the school system as an instrument to" raise" the standards of Southern society. Schools had to be brought under the control of centralized administration. One-room schools, which were a bastion of local control and of parental involvement in education, were inimical to reform goals.

That alteration, however, was not quickly accomplished since there were still 985 one-teacher schools operating in Virginia in 1950. (They disappeared by 1985, though Dewalt records "no data" kept by the Virginia State Department of Education as to the final year when one-room schools operated there.)[20] The intersectionalist reformers were cognizant of the attachment of local people to these schools:

> The one-room school, wrote the authors of one manual of reform, was "so deeply rooted in the hearts of the people . . . [and] so much a part of their mental constitution, that it will not be given up without a struggle."[21]

There were obvious reasons for people's devotion to the one-room, one-teacher schools. First, those schools were not standardized. While most of them looked generally alike, each of them in both overt and subtle ways reflected the character of its community. School populations were made up of the children of families from the area directly surrounding the schools.[22] Therefore, all students' early school years must have been spent in familiar surroundings with other members of their own families. "The school housed the activities that joined people into a community, and the identity of rural communities became inextricably linked with their schools."[23]

The one-room, one-teacher school in Virginia was seen as a "blight" by the northern philanthropists led by Robert Curtis Ogden and John D. Rockefeller who set out in the first decades of the century to raise the standards of Southern culture to those of the North. Since one-room schools represented local control, their elimination was an important goal for the Co-operative Education Board, the agency of reform. It was a goal that was not finally realized until long after it was conceived. Whether or not that goal was justified is not a consideration of this study. The purpose of this study was to determine if, along with the elimination of those heterogeneous though preponderantly segregated one-room schools, might have also been eliminated much that was valuable to the educational process. The educational reformers—urban educators, intersectionalists, and urban civic groups—who saw the need to eliminate the one-room schools had perceptions of those schools which were very different from those of the community members, students, and teachers to whom those schools belonged:

> Because school reformers were imbued with a cultural imperiousness common to their era, they examined rural society exclusively on their own, highly subjective terms. The result was a mixture of rich description and distorted analysis, an obsession with detailed description combined with conclusions shaped by their own experience. Through a perspective that was both highly empirical and highly subjective, reformers agreed that the main problem with rural education was its close symbiosis with rural society.[24]

Gulliford portrays the perceptions of community members, students, and teachers differently:

> The legacy of the one-room school for southern blacks was not the well-furnished, white-clapboard structures of New England, but the sense of community, of belonging to a family of children and their larger families, was the same for country school students and teachers of any race, in any state.[25]

Fostering of personal growth, ownership of one's learning, and community feeling were characteristics of the one-room school experience reflected in the interviews which form the basis of this study as well as my 1989 research project. Marian Cramer, discussing country schools in South Dakota, said, "If we examine what was good, what was useful in the one-room school and translate this to our modern educational system, we shall have achieved a great deal."[26] My book examines what was effective in the one-room schools of one rural Virginia county and suggests the possibility of transferring these attributes to modern schooling.

Chapter Two presents a review of literature relevant to this study. It provides 1) contextual information for the study, 2) methodological models for it, and 3) relevant current theory or models. Chapter Three presents a comparison of the material from two of the respondents who represent both ends of the racial continuum into which my respondents fit. Coincidentally, the origins of these two men also represent both ends of my respondents' socio-economic continuum. I have made the comparison in order to demonstrate the fact that the one-room school experience was similar at both extremes of these continuums, racial and socio-economic. Chapter Four presents an evocation of the ambiance of Buckingham County's one-room schools. The evocation is effected through groups of excerpts from the respondents' writings and interviews comprising the majority of the study's data. The format in which they are presented is similar to that used by Studs Terkel in *Hard Times: An Oral History of America in the Depression*[27] and *American Dreams: Lost and Found.*[28] That format is particularly suited to this study because it gives the reader direct access to the "voices" of my respondents in the same way that Terkel wished to allow the reader such access. Chapter Five's excerpts are collected under headings which are the themes used as titles of categories representing various aspects of my respondents' educational experience. This rubric of category titles resulted from analysis of the study's data. The titles around which I have arranged these voices are these:

A. On Schoolhouses
B. About Schooldays
C. Of Pedagogy
D. On Writing
E. About Reading
F. On Speaking
G. On Listening
H. Of "A Roomful of Teachers"
I. On the School Family
J. On Community Relationships
K. About Memorable Occasions
L. Of Disparity and Adversity
M. Of What Was Good and Useful

The assemblages of excerpts in Chapter Five permit the reader to perceive the ambiance of the one-room schools. My interpretive descriptions of the data provided by those excerpts follow each assemblage. In Chapter Six, I present an analysis of "A Gathering of Teachers." This gathering, comprised of four of my respondents, was held and videotaped on April 10, 1990, at the Buckingham County home of Mrs. Dorothy Anderson Morgan, one of the four respondents. These four people met to consider the possibility of reinventing effective one-room school characteristics within the constraints of modern education. All four respondents, educators experienced in one-room schools either as students, as teachers, or as both, are also experienced as educators in more modern education. The conversation which resulted from their meeting became one which focused on the obstacles to the reinvention of effective one-room schooling characteristics.

Chapter Six is my discussion of the conclusions and implications of the study and of the directions further research might take. I suggest experimentation in reorganization of existing educational structures and study of long-term, multi-level learning teams. I also suggest construction of a theoretical model from which to train teachers for long-term classrooms. Last, I suggest further naturalistic inquiry into one-room schools. The study is supplemented by three appendices. Appendix One presents the demographics of those interviewed for this study. The interview protocols make up Appendix II, and Appendix II contains the instructions for the respondents' timed writings which extended some of the interviews as well as d the release form.

Notes

1. National Committee on Excellence in Education. *A Nation At Risk: The Imperative for Educational Reform* (Washington, D.C.: U.S. Government, 1983).

2. Wikipedia, s.v. *No Child Left Behind Act,* http://en.wikipedia. org /wiki; http://www.ed.gov/policy/elsec/leg/esea02/index.html.

3. Sandra Nichols, "The Federal Government's No Child Left Behind Act (NCLB — dubbed 'nicklebee')," April 26, 2003, *When NCLB Standards Meet Reality,* tellingthetruth.com.

4. Clerk of the House of Representatives, "Final vote results for roll-call 145." May 23, 2001. http://clerk.house .gov/evs/2001/roll145.xml

5. Diane Ravitch, *American Educator,* (Summer 2010), http:// www. aft. org/ pdfs/ americaneducator/summer2010/Ravitch.pdf

6. Ravitch, *American Educator.*

7. E.D. Hirsch, Jr., *Cultural Literacy: What Every American Needs to Know* (New York, NY: Houghton-Mifflin Company, 1987).

8. Allen Bloom, *The Closing of the American Mind: How Higher Education Has Failed Democracy And Impoverished The Souls of Today's Students,* (New York: Simon and Schuster, 1987).

9. http://nces.ed.gov/NAAL/kf_demographics.asp

10. Jonathan Kozol, *Illiterate America,* (Garden City, NJ: Anchor Press/Doubleday, 1985).

11. Mark Dewalt, "One-Room Schools in the United States" (Paper presented at the meeting of the Eastern Educational Research Association, Savannah, GA, February 24, 1989).

12. William A. Link, *A Hard Country and a Lonely Place: Schooling, Society, and Reform in Rural Virginia, 1870-1920* (Chapel Hill, NC: University of NorthCarolina Press, 1986), 30-45.

13. Link, *A Hard Country,* 73-74.

14. Link, *A Hard Country,* 76.

15. Link, *A Hard Country,* 113.

16. Link, *A Hard Country,* 85-87.

17. Link, *A Hard Country,* 88-89.

18. Link, *A Hard Country,* 141.

19. Link, *A Hard Country,* 148.

20. Dewalt, "One-Room Schools," 12.

21. Link, *A Hard Country,* Link, 143.

22. Andrew Gulliford, *America's Country Schools* (Washington, D.C.: Preservation Press; 1984), 47.

23. Gulliford, *America's Country Schools,* 35.

24. Link, *A Hard Country,* 90.

25. Gulliford, *America's Country Schools,* 106.

26. Cited in Gulliford. *America's Country Schools,* 125.

27. Studs Terkel, *Hard Times: An Oral History of America in the Depression,* (New York: Pantheon Books, 1966).

28. Studs Terkel, *American Dreams: Lost and Found,* (New York: Pantheon Books, 1980).

Chapter Two
A Review of Relevant Literature

The literature selected for review in this section is organized into three sections: studies treating one-room schools as they existed earlier in this and in the last century, (historiography, memoirs and interview, and quantitative description); studies treating one-room schools as they existed later in the 20th century; and relevant theory and models. The criteria for selection of the included literature were: its provision of contextual information for this study, methodological models for it, and theory connected to it. The study's research question wasaimed at producing an idiographic exploration of one-room schooling earlier in this century in a specific location. Naturalistic, idiographic studies offer readers transferability from the analysis of data which is context-bound. This literature survey has influenced many of my decisions as a naturalistic researcher by suggesting directions from which to analyze one-room schooling in the particular time and place encompassed by this study.

Studies Treating One-Room Schools as They Existed Earlier in This and in the Last Century:

1. Historiography

There have been many historiographical studies on one-room schools. William A. Link's book, *A Hard Country and A Lonely Place,*[1] is a thorough historiography of society, rural education, and reform in Virginia which encompasses the years 1870-1920. It perforce included one-room, one-teacher schools since they were a major target for reform of the Southern Education Board (SEB), later the Co-operative Education Association (CEA). They were uniquely representative of the local control which the SEB felt had to be broken if its reform plans were to be effective. Link records the denigration of the one-room situation by agents of reform; they stressed the impermanence of the school buildings, the transitory aspects of the population of teachers, and the fact that teachers were often hired by the local populace rather than a centralized administration. All of these were in fact true, but they were not strong enough invalidations to warrant closing the one-room schools. They were compensated for by such qualities as the family-like ambiance of the schools.

Link drew on a number of documents which included discussions of one-room schools. Such documents as A. C. Monahan's *The Status of Rural Education in the United* States[2] and Edgar W. Knight's *Public Education in the South*[3] were important sources for him. A major source was *A History of Education in Virginia* by Cornelius J. Heatwole.[4] Such sources have been valuable to this study in terms of context.

My study is informed primarily by reports from living people about the one-room school in the decades after 1920. In 1981, many such reports were published as a result of a huge research effort that encompassed several states in the West—Wyoming, Utah, Kansas, Colorado, North Dakota, South Dakota, and Arkansas among them. This project was funded by the National Endowment for the Humanities and sponsored by the Mountain Plains Library Association based in Silt, Colorado, under the title *Country School Legacy: Humanities on the Frontier*.[5] This research effort was aimed at studying the role that one-teacher, one-room schools played in the history of the frontier, and locating and preserving information related to country schools.

Among the twelve reports, there are 1049 pages of materials which deal with various topics. They display a large variety of subject matter and of forms. Among them are anecdotes, interviews, surveys, comparisons of schools as they were to current times, investigations of sexual biases toward female teachers, a report on the architectural characteristics of one-room schools in Kansas, school census figures, autobiographies, and discussions of multiple uses of the school buildings. The compilation of materials and artifacts is housed in Silt, Colorado.

Although the titles of the individual reports deal with various historical aspects of the Western one-room schools when they were a major means of delivering education, there is no evidence that the data in these reports have been analyzed for insights valuable to modern education. Instead, the reports explore titles like "Work and Leisure in Country Schools in Wyoming,"[6] "Schoolmarms of Utah: Separate But Unequal,"[7] and "The Young Citizens League: Its Origins and Development in South Dakota to 1930,"[8] or, they compile the data gathered in the separate states and categorize six aspects of rural education—country schools as community centers, country schools as historical sites, country schools and the Americanization of ethnic groups, the country school curriculum (reading, writing, and arithmetic), teachers (their roles, rules, restrictions), and the country school today. These six aspects were used as organizational headings in most of the reports. *The Country School Legacy: Humanities on the Frontier* research has been used as a base for other publications. Examples are Gulliford[9] on the architecture and restoration of Western country schools, and Grundy[10] on the country school as represented in literature.

The relevance of this research effort to my study lies more in its subject matter than in any other aspect of it. It is an attempt to preserve the past without analysis; my study attempts to preserve the past but also move beyond it to suggest ways that its lessons might inform the present. Three other relevant historiographical studies of one-room schools concern southern locales. Williams[11] traces the history of West Virginia one-room schools into the 1970's. His study describes demographically various aspects of that history such as teachers, buildings, curriculum, and length of school year. Tierney[12] explores three periods in the history of education in Big Laurel, West Virginia, and the effects of that history on the community. Rice[13] chronicles the closing of one of Kentucky's last remaining one-room schools at the end of the 1986-87 school year amidst protest from the community.

Another such study is Daniel Tysen Smith's dissertation done at the University of Kentucky.[14] It is a case study of the one-room school at Jacob's Creek in Floyd County, Kentucky, which was closed at the July, 1987, meeting of the Floyd County School Board. Smith's study has as its sub-theme the question of the advantages and disadvantages of the consolidated school as opposed to the community school. His analysis reveals advantages and disadvantages of one-room schools which are depicted as being similar in some respects to those revealed by my study. For example, the community at Jacob's Creek felt close ties to their school, the variety of ages and ability levels in the school allowed for "much tutoring and sharing of ideas," flexibility allowed for "spontaneous teaching and learning to take place," the "natural flow of ideas can take place unhindered by time constraints," and there was a "climate of affection and harmony" in the school which fostered a sense of belonging and individual acceptance. These advantages were offset by the limited personnel, the shortage of supplies, and the adjustment students had to make when they went on to a large high school.[15]

These four studies are nearer geographically to mine, though only Smith's employs naturalistic methodologies. My study produced insights useful to modern education through analysis of naturalistic data for its transferability to modern schooling. Neither Smith's nor the other three present any consideration of such transferability. Swanson's study[16] is much larger but similar to these four. It is a collection of several kinds of materials about one-room schools, especially in Illinois. It traces their history from 1825 and relates anecdotes and legends about them, but provides no data analysis for those characteristics that might be reinvented in modern schooling.

2. Memoirs and Interviews

Memoirs and interviews are comparable to the raw data of my study, and their content suggests areas which I wanted to explore with my respondents. "Echoes of Spring Valley" is a privately published memoir by J. Clarine J. Boyken [sic].[17] In it, the author narrates her experiences as a student and a member of the "secure community life centered in the one-room Spring Valley

School in Hamilton County, Iowa, in the early decades of the century." Mrs. Boyken offers specific details: the dry sandwich in the lunchpail in the pre-waxpaper era, the recitation bench to which children were called for class sessions, the double desks shared with a seatmate, the open classroom where older pupils were always available to help beginners, and the annual visit of the school superintendent. Such specific details evoke the ambiance of Mrs. Boyken's one-room school in the same manner as my study evokes ambiance.

Other student memoirs include Wendell H. Howard's "Progressing Education."[18] The author, an educator, characterizes his teacher as having employed a style that maintained excellent discipline, fostered self-confidence in students, drew significant lessons from everyday experience, and developed the whole person. Norman D. Anderson's "I Remember Springdale School"[19] concentrates on individualized instruction and the pride that alumni of one-room schools feel in their experience. "My First Year at School, 1895"[20] targets the author's memories of the physical surroundings in an Iowa school. These memoirs reflect the type of data which forms the basis of my study, but offer no analysis.

Two books by Jesse Stuart, *To Teach, To Love*[21] and *The Thread That Runs So True,*[22] fictionalize memoirs. These books are based on the story of Stuart's experience as a one-room school teacher in the remote hills of Kentucky. Stuart started teaching in Kentucky at 17, and he records learning with his students in a very real way. Jesse Stuart went on to become a widely-known lecturer, teacher, and important regional writer. His books analyze the raw data of his experience and make that experience into a story which emphasizes the fact that both teacher and students were learners in the one-room school community. This element of the "teacher-student learning community" is one which emerged from my research.

A document which exemplifies the methodology I used in my research is the record edited by Dropkin[23] of an interview which Arthur Tobier conducted in June of 1974 for presentation at the "Roots of Open Education in America Conference" held in New York on April 12, 1975. The interview respondent is Marian Brooks, a distinguished teacher who began her career in 1924 at 15 in a one-room New Hampshire school. The interview describes an emphasis on child-centered, informal learning situations born out of the necessity to facilitate learning in a one-room, one-teacher school and to utilize integrated grade levels, family/community resources, and family/community involvement.

I found the interview protocol in this document useful as a model for my own. Its questions covered these subjects:

1. nature of the early teacher preparatory program
2. involvement and interaction between the teacher and the community
3. composition of the community
4. relationship between student and teacher
5. development of the curriculum and curriculum guidelines
6. models for child development
7. common educational activities
8. physical facilities

    9. academic assessment

    10. school district policies

    11. administrative ,philosophy and procedure

    12. interaction between teachers in the district

    13. salaries   ·

    14. differences between various early educational philosophies

    15. child-centered vs.learning-centered approach to education (Dropkin)

I formed questions based on these areas of concern to make up my interview protocol, and referred to it as a checklist when analyzing data for this study.

3. Quantitative Description

In an unpublished paper presented to the annual Eastern Educational Research Association meeting in 1989, Mark Dewalt[24] quantified the distribution of public and private one-room schools in the United States. He recorded 27,792 such schools in 1950 in 22 states where data were available. He recorded 985 operating in Virginia as of 1950. In 1985, he recorded 749 operating in the whole country, but none of those were in Virginia. By 1987, the number had dropped to 674 in the country and was still zero in Virginia.[25] The Fall Membership Records for Virginia's public schools collated by the Virginia Department of Education in 1988-89 showed five schools with a population less than fifty. One of these was an alternative school in Alexandria, and another was a special education program in Giles County. In Virginia, then, the one-room school is indeed a thing of the past. The passing of one-room schools in the South is recorded in another article. In "One-Teacher Schools in the States of the Old Confederacy,"[26] the Southern Education Reporting Service chronicles the disappearance of one-room schools in seventeen Southern and border states because of consolidation. Also, it discusses the advantages and disadvantages of the practice of consolidation.

"Educational Achievements of One-Teacher and of Larger Rural Schools"[27] provides a synthesis of studies prior to that year; these studies focus on academic achievement in rural schools as measured by standardized tests. Covert presents comparative statistics for reading, arithmetic, spelling, and handwriting. The results show that students in larger rural schools achieve higher academically than students from one-room schools. The validity of this study, however, is suspect. The selection principles used for the studies included are not coherent, (e.g., reading scores for twenty states, but spelling scores for only five). The kinds of scores used were not homogeneous, (e.g., median spelling scores in the state of Wisconsin and raw spelling scores from Spokane County, Washington). Therefore, the results of the study cannot be interpreted as a valid denigration of the effectiveness of one-room, one-teacher schools in the era encompassed by the study.

Studies Treating One-Room Schools as They Currently Exist

A second category of literature relevant to this study encompasses the one-room school of the present era. Outside the United States, the one-teacher school as a mode for delivery of education is still major in some areas. Examples are Australia and New Zealand. Two articles dealing with one-teacher, one-room schooling in Australia and New Zealand discuss curriculum development in the Australian one-teacher schools of the 1980's.[28] An earlier analytical article presented some empirical research into the conditions affecting learning in those one-teacher schools. Nash et al.[29] examined the breadth and quality of the curriculum in those schools, patterns of friendship, economic constraints, and the school in the social life of the community.

These research categories are related to the interview protocols which this study will employ. All three of these articles inform my study by characterizing modern one-room, one-teacher schools. They are different from the one-room schools of the past. They attempt to conform to nationally normative patterns of schooling rather than to local needs.

Noteworthy literature treating one-room, one-teacher schools of the present era in the United States continues to reveal differences. Muse et al.[30] is one example. The first chapter of this monograph is an overview of the history of the one-room school in 20th century American education. The second is descriptive and demographic information on the surviving one-room schools based on studies done between 1984-87 (e.g., Hughes[31]). Chapter 3 is a comparison between current one-room schools and their counterparts in the 1960's. Chapter 4 describes selected schools, and the fifth chapter describes the architectural evolution of these schools. The sixth and last chapter recapitulates and speculates on the dim future of these one-room schools.

An earlier publication (Muse et al.[32]) is an investigation of the secondary performance of 204 secondary students who had attended rural one-teacher schools in Nebraska, South Dakota, and Montana. Data gathered from students, teachers, and administrators indicates that these students were academically similar to other students but had difficulty adjusting socially to boarding in town. Both Muse et al. (1985) and Muse et al. (1987) attempt to assure the reader that one-room schools of the present era can measure up to the national standards, employ nationally approved curricula and methodologies, and are educationally effective by the measures of such effectiveness currently employed. They are pictured as being, in effect, centrally controlled schoolrooms which just happen to be separate from a larger building.

Bruce Barker[33] (1984, 1986a, 1986b) presents demographic information on 402 one-room school teachers yielding profiles of those teachers and some characteristics of their schools. (e.g., average size [11], average time spent on individualized instruction [90%]). Barker and Muse[34] published a short article which traces the decline of the numbers of one-room schools in the United States and draws on Mr. Barker's survey to describe the characteristics of the current one-room schools implying that the disadvantages accruing from their decentralization far outweigh any advantages which may accrue from close association with their communities.

Also, Cousins,[35] Scott[36] and Gardener[37] are all writings which dwell on the drawbacks of one-room schools in the 80's, citing such things as overworked teachers, lack of access to the mainstream of nationally approved educational methods, and limited funding.

Two other articles on one-room, one-teacher schools in specific regions present a different emphasis (Alkire,[38] Kindley[39]). They stress the advantages of these schools to teachers, students, and parents. Examples of these advantages are convenience to the homes of students and teachers, availability of the school building for use by the immediate community, and ease of facilitation of parental involvement in children's education.

These studies of the nation's surviving one-room schools, then, present a picture with some confusing features. Some studies present a positive portrait (Alkire[40]); other studies present negative aspects of the schools (Muse et al.[41]). All of them depict single classrooms reflecting standardization rather than schools which express the unique character of their communities. My study examined the one-room schools of a different time for an expression of unique community character. The data on which it is based suggest how a unique community character worked to the advantage of students, teachers, and parents and how the redevelopment of more specific community character for schools might be advantageous to modern education.

There are some areas of the United States where more attention is paid to the one-room school than in others. Several pieces of literature suggest that that attention may not be directed toward making one-room schools in these areas reflections of national norms, but rather schools which reflect the needs of their communities. Even though Dewalt[42] lists only 20 such schools in Alaska in 1987, an article by Marilyn K. Johnson et al.[43] describes training seminars in coping with a wide range of abilities offered by specifically discussed agencies for teachers and teacher-aides in Alaskan one-teacher schools.

Three articles are devoted to teacher preparation for the one-teacher school. Blackwood[44] in "More Like A School Family Than Just a Teacher and His/Her Students. Is a One-teacher School for You? . ." gives beginning teachers in Alaskan one-room schools some practical advice about teaching and living in the isolated Alaskan communities. Bruce Miller[45] discusses the apparent lack of content in teacher preparation programs nationwide for teaching in one-teacher schools but does point out nine rural preservice and inservice programs in Hawaii, Alaska, Oregon, Montana, Utah, and British Columbia. The four Alaskan programs focus on one-room schools in remote native villages. A last article presents the results of a survey of rural teachers, one-room teachers among them, as information for the Rural Effective Schools Project. Kleinfeld and McDiarmid[46] report that rural Alaskan teachers did not frequently use nationally recommended teaching practices. They used hands-on and self-paced instruction, and they assigned very little homework. These Alaskan schools, then, are apparently not making that effort mentioned earlier (e.g., Muse et al.,[47] Muse et al.,[48] Barker & Muse[49]) to be standardized single classrooms offering nationally approved curricula and adhering to national norms. Rather, their effort is more like that of the one-room schools of the past—to serve the specific needs and character of their communities.

The positive qualities inherent in the one-room situations in the past (e. g., the necessity for peer teaching and for teacher and students to be a community of teachers and learners) are sometimes devalued as being disadvantages, if they exist at all in the surviving one-room schools. My study does not assume their value; rather, it scrutinizes such characteristics to determine their effectiveness.

In an unpublished dissertation, Jeanne Masson-Douglas[50] has proposed translation of one characteristic of one-room schools both past and present into modern schooling. She started with the proposition that "conditions common to small rural school environments are likely to influence learning in positive ways."[51] Masson-Douglas used data collected from 181 students, 14 teachers, and 98 parents connected with 14 public one-room schools operating in New England in 1980-81. The data revealed the perceptions of these people concerning the learning environment in those schools, the organization of instructional settings in them, and the nature of student interaction in those settings. Masson-Douglas focused on size as one of the characteristics of present era New England one-room schools which positively influences learning. Small size, of course, has always been a characteristic of one-room schools. Her study suggests mine in its advancement of three "action proposals": 1) cross- age interactions within schools; 2) connections between intentional and incidental learning; and 3) a commonality of curriculum while maintaining individualization of instruction. Masson-Douglas has set a precedent of a kind for my study by her evaluation of these characteristics, which she sees as inherently characteristic of one-room schools, as worth including in modern education. My study similarly attempts to articulate characteristics which could be reinvented in modern schooling.

There is a small body of literature concerning one-teacher schools in the present era which presents a picture quite different from that dealing with the surviving public one-room schools. It is literature concerned with private one-room schools. Three notable articles concern "Old-Order Mennonite" or "Old-Order Amish" schools. The Amish have been assertive about defending their way of life which subsumes their educational practices. Dewalt and Troxell[52] performed a "Case Study of an Old-Order Mennonite One-Room School" which concluded that the Mennonite heritage permeated the school, a heritage stressing literacy and the need for hard work. They used interviews, the Flanders interaction analysis, and the Cooper observation system (a combination of quantitative and qualitative methods) to collect data. Their study relates to mine strongly in the approach aimed at ascertaining the specific character of a school. Though I did not have a presently existing situation as they did, my study depicts, as they did, the ambiance and character of the schools I investigated. Their case study, however, makes no attempt to identify elements of the situation which could profitably be translated and reinvented in public schooling as mine does.

Amish schools have also been studied by Marlow Ediger.[53] "Old-Order Amish and the Philosophy of Education" is a characterization of the current Amish culture and schooling, which is outside the mainstream of American culture. The conditions in the one-room schools which are their only method of delivering education are very much like those in the one-room schools in all of America earlier in this century and in the nineteenth century. Ediger[54] reports a study in which 23 students from an Amish school took the Iowa Test of Basic Skills during 1979. Fifteen of the 23 ranked over 50% in the language arts subtests. Both of the eighth graders in the group, (eighth grade is the last year of Amish schooling) ranked over 90% overall.

These studies of the Old-Order Amish suggest an approach to education effective even by nationally advocated standards. That suggestion has ramifications for other educators and for policy makers. My study does not deal with currently existing situations, but the fact that these Amish schools are effective supports suggestions in my study of reinventing similar characteristics from one-room schools.

Relevant Current Theory and Models

This third category of relevant literature is not comprised of studies about various aspects of one-room schools. Rather it includes theory and models from three prominent contemporary educators which connect either overtly or by construction to the kind of education that once was offered by the one-room school.

Daniel Fader, William Glasser, and Paulo Friere are a disparate trio in most ways, yet one with a commonality significant to my study. All three stress that education must be an undertaking which originates in the individual classroom among the group of people who are its members rather than the superimposing of a curriculum from "somewhere else" on both the teacher and the students. My study, in its investigation of the experience of people involved in the one-room schools of Buckingham County, Virginia, shows that this proposition emerges as a defining characteristic of its one-room schools.

Daniel Fader is the author of a program which he has called "Hooked on Books." In the 1976 edition[55] of his book by the same name, he makes many references to the one-room school. Fader's book is subtitled "How to Learn and How to Teach Reading and Writing With Pleasure." The articulation of the "Hooked on Books" program originated in Fader's experiences in shaping and testing a curriculum for the teaching of English at the W. J. Maxey Training School at Whitmore Lake, Michigan. Fader himself was an English professor at the University of Michigan at that time. His specialty was Renaissance British literature, so his participation in the shaping of a program for teaching English to a group of boys at a reform school was unorthodox.

That unorthodoxy was highly productive. The work at W. J. Maxey Training School involved a population of students who were not "performance-
oriented" and for whom there was a need "to perceive an immediate relationship
between cause and effect" before they would be "successfully motivated."[56]
That work produced a program which took "the child's attitude as its primary,
and sometimes its sole, object."[57] It was a reading and writing across the curriculum program, although it was articulated before that group of words became so
commonly used in education.

However, its principles are equally apropos for a student population which
is in fact "performance-oriented," and thus for the whole school population. The
program resembles those of the one-room schools I investigated in 1989 by
making learning the primary concern.

The component of Daniel Fader's program which leads him to make fre-
quent references to the one-room school era is his idea for learning groups. In
the chapter "A Classroom Full of Teachers," Fader commences with a discussion of the influence of television on the student. His comments are that we cannot know the effects of "a thousand hours a year" of television watching and that
we are probably dealing with students whose intellect is different from any we
have before encountered because of that time spent watching. He characterizes
the effects as a "social isolation" which imprisons, just as illiteracy does, the
person inside the walls of self. "If six hours a day of television in their homes is
making isolated voyeurs of our students, then we must change our style of teaching to meet the needs of a new clientele."[58] Fader then suggests that the "anti-
dote" for the "slow poison" of social isolation might be found by looking at the
one-room school situation. He says that the one-room schools developed a great
strength to compensate for their great weakness. Their demise was caused by the
fact that populations of children became too large to be accommodated in the
one-room facility which brought the need for consolidation and expansion. He
says, however, that the critical growth point was defined not by how many students one teacher could teach, but rather by how many students the schoolroom
could hold. So far as I can tell from extensive inquiry, no teacher who taught in
a one-room schoolhouse ever experienced the luxury of class size limited by her
capacity to meet the educational needs of her students.[59]

The great strength that the one-room school teacher had to develop to compensate for the school's weakness was to become "in fact both a teacher and a
supervisor of many teachers who were themselves students in her classroom."[60]
Fader's point here is a critical one. He predicates a learning environment quite
different from the one familiar in modern classrooms where the teacher is the
disseminator of knowledge and the students receivers of that knowledge. Instead, he points out the fact that the one-room school was a teaching-learning
community where learning was owned by all the members. Fader continues with
a quote from an interview with two one-room school teachers. In response to his
asking how they had survived with no training and no professional support, they
said that the children had to help them. Older children taught younger ones,
quicker children helped slower ones. They admitted that it had to do with self-

discipline then taught at home, but it had much more to do with the fact that every child was looked after by at least one other one. "No one got lost" inside the classroom, and that included the teacher who did not have to feel the guilt that teachers often express now about not being able to deal with the students they must seat in their classrooms every day. Nor did they express frustrations in the form of questions about what to do with a heterogeneous classroom.[61]

Fader then discusses the second part of the lesson that was lost with the one-room school's demise: Lost also was the knowledge that all teachers possess from their own experience, the knowledge that understanding more often accompanies the act of teaching than any other act of the human intellect. Knowing that, knowing also that we cannot teach or touch every student ourselves, we have nevertheless failed to use the students in our classes to teach the students in our classes.[62] In 1976, Fader had for six years been using the principles of peer teaching in his own pedagogy by setting up learning groups and, he says, "Nothing in my teaching experience has ever worked so invariably or so well."[63]

The next interesting discussion in Fader relevant to my study is a section dealing with the use of speaking in the one-room schools. Many people he has interviewed remember learning from listening to lessons being recited or from reciting their own. In recalling those days when voices were more valued than silence in the classroom, a woman who does not teach put words to the most interesting and significant memory I've heard, "If I didn't learn anything else, I learned that what I said was alright!" What an extraordinary lesson![64]

Fader advocates a restoration of the oral component to the teaching of language arts as well as to the teaching of all other subjects. He says that students' single most reliable source of language is their own voice. In the teaching of writing, he requires students to read their work aloud before handing it in, and to read it aloud to the members of their learning groups so that they have the added benefit of two more pairs of ears.

Daniel Fader's program is based on a model that he conceived from what he had learned about one-room schools. It is a model that is implicit in the work of William Glasser, M.D. Glasser's book, *Control Theory in the Classroom* articulates a program called "co-operative" learning.[65] The program that he has devised is also a plan for using learning teams. In his control theory of behavior, Glasser offers a theoretical base for his plan which is contrary to "stimulus-response" theories of behavior. According to Glasser, all behavior is an attempt to satisfy present needs. His needs list is heterarchical and recursive. He cites five needs: to stay alive and reproduce; to belong; to have power; to have freedom; and to have fun. Glasser posits these five needs as genetically imprinted in all humans, and he characterizes a "good school" as a place where students believe that if they do some work, they will be able to satisfy these needs enough so that it makes sense to go on working.[66] Glasser asserts that the motivation to satisfy these needs comes from within ourselves and not from without. This is why learning situations where teachers dispense information in accordance with a prescribed curriculum do not work for a majority of the students presently in our schools. Fifty percent of them make grades that allow them to succeed; the other fifty percent do not even try to learn what is offered through such curricula.[67]

Glasser's plan to restructure our schools is based on learning teams. He devotes Chapter 4 of his book to the idea of "learning pictures" which either allow students to effectively perform, or block students from effectively performing learning activities. In it, he introduces the idea of "pictures" of students grouped together to create and construct assignments and then to implement those assignments. In Chapter 7, he introduces the component which makes his plan different from Fader's. He uses the model of business in which the teacher is manager. Where Fader's idea is of the teacher as supervisor, Glasser's is of the teacher as a manager of teams. The element of competition, which Glasser sees as deriving from the "power" need, is an important part of his model. His model consists of learning teams, all of which can win. This is a plan designed to change the self-image of the student from "loser" to "winner." Glasser cites the use of competition by Robert Slavin of Johns Hopkins in Slavin's work on cooperative learning.[68] Glasser says that both he and Slavin recommend the use of competition after the learning team relationships are established in the classroom.

The relevance of Glasser's *Control Theory in the Classroom* to my study is that it places the locus of the instructional plan within the given classroom group. Also, it fosters caring among students about a goal they have themselves articulated. Working toward that common goal tends to make it possible that a learning team would care about each other. Glasser's model suggests the importance of investigating the kind of instructional environment that existed in the one-room, one-teacher school. The overt use of Glasser's theory has mostly disappeared in 2010. A resurgence of its use on a national basis is unlikely. It has, however, morphed into many other collaborative models. Multiliteracies theory enfolds it. Distance and digital learning ride on collaboration. Wikipedia's article on Glasser lists the Glasser Institute that is quite functional in 2010. Glasser is alive at the present date and published last in 2007.[69]

Both Glasser and Fader write against the concept of "tracking" as destructive to the co-operative dimension which they both see as essential to education. Tracking, as practiced through 1990, is a concept which was not part of the lexicon of the one-room school. Neither is tracking a part of the pedagogical lexicon of Paulo Freire. Freire's pedagogical principles, endorsed in the United States by educational theorists such as Ann Berthoff and Henri Giroux, seem to be most trenchantly like the principles that made the early one-room schools work.

Paulo Freire was a Brazilian educator whose work was in bringing literacy to the masses in Third World countries. For that work, he suffered persecution from those whose interests he thwarted by educating Brazil's disenfranchised population. For that work, also, he gained worldwide recognition. *Literacy: Reading the Word and the World*[70] book co-authored with Donaldo Macedo, is one of several in which his pedagogical principles are articulated. Paulo Freire and assistants trained by him used methodologies by which they have taught people to read and write in as little as forty hours.

Freire's methodology is predicated on the students' experience in "reading the world," by which Freire means students' ability to talk about and interpret the world around them. In subsequently "reading the word," by which Freire means learning what groups of letters make words that match their concepts of the world, they use both word and world recursively to extend their experience of both. Freire and his assistants use a visualization process of a text which is a list of key words produced by each group of people who are the learners. Each group writes and draws what Freire calls a "Culture Circle Notebook" in which what is named and pictured is the life experience of the group. Thus each group's text for achieving literacy is an invention of the group, and each group's achievement of literacy is a reinvention of method. The dialectical and dialogic nature of the learning process enables both teacher and student to learn from each other as they function as a community of discoverers. All are students and all are teachers of each other. Friere's methods are instances of "co-operative learning" (Glasser;[71] Slavin[72]) because both students and teachers are learners through co-operative dialogue. Education is a process that takes place inside the learner through the dialogic participation in a group of learners who together ascertain what it is that they know and what it is they need to know. Education is not the dissemination by a teacher of a curriculum from somewhere else which may not be relevant but which must be memorized by learners as prescribed.

The concepts articulated by Fader, Glasser, and Freire suggest connections to a time in the history of American education when the one-room, one-teacher school was a major educational mode where pedagogy was differently practiced from today. In his own pedagogical practice, Fader reinvented an effective characteristic of one-room schooling, peer teaching. He was teaching in a modern school, and so he set a precedent for such reinvention. He attested to peer teaching's working both "invariably" and "well."[73]

Glasser uses the same concept, peer teaching, as the basis for his "learning teams." Glasser's program would probably be more aptly termed an adaptation then a reinvention since he uses business competition as his metaphor.

Freire, who was a South American, probably did not knowingly model his pedagogy on effective characteristics of North American one-room, one-teacher schooling. That pedagogy, however, is startlingly similar to one-room schooling as it is characterized in this study. Freire, too, taught in modern schools, reinventing effective one-room schooling characteristics. Whether or not he is overtly conscious of doing so, he is. In teaching the peasants in Third-World countries to read through the "word-world" connection, his pedagogy provided new possibilities for application of those characteristics.

While this is not its major purpose, my study incidentally provides an additional kind of validity for the ideas of these three theorists.

Summary

The literature encompassed in this review is organized into three sections. These sections are: studies treating one-room schools as they existed earlier in this and the last century; studies treating one-room schools as they exist in the present era; and relevant current theory and models.

The first category of literature, studies treating one-room schools as they existed earlier in this century and the last one provides contextual background to my study as well as furnishes some methodological models in interviews and memoirs. It also reveals a dearth of analysis of the kind which this study provides, analysis to yield insights about characteristics from the one-room schooling of the past which could be worth translation and reinvention in the present.

The studies in the second category, one-room schools as they existed in 1989, also provide contextual background which will furnish points of reference for comparing the characteristics of surviving public and private one-room schools to those which emerge from my research. In addition, these studies furnish methodological models. They also reflect a dearth of the kind of analysis provided by this study for they number only one attempt to discern elements which it might be advantageous to reinvent in all modern schooling.

The third category of literature, relevant current theory and models, consists of current theory and models which. either overtly as demonstrated by Fader or by construction as demonstrated by Glasser and Freire, connect to elements which were part of the one-room school. Fader represents a reinvention of one particular element of one-room schooling, peer teaching, applied to the language arts. Glasser and Freire do not evince the same degree of awareness of the characteristics of one-room schooling, but the principles articulated in their programs bear a trenchant likeness to some of those characteristics. My study enlarges upon these connections to clarify and/or validate them.

As a major method of delivery of education in America, the one-room school has been eliminated. In 2010, there are a very few still operating, six, for example, in Huron County, Michigan. Twenty-first century one-room schools are, of course, completely hooked into the rest of the district electronically. William Link has told the story of why the one-room school was eliminated in Virginia and the rest of the South. It was a bastion of local and parental control in rural education which stood in the way of the reform that represented progress in the judgment of those who represented the dominant culture of the time, people like John D. Rockefeller and Robert Curtis Ogden, as well as Jabez Lamar Monroe Curry and Edwin Alderman. It was not my suggestion in this study that we could return to the one-room, one-teacher school as it existed earlier in this century. Rather, I sought to answer my research question: "How can the experiences of people who taught in and/or went to one-room, one-teacher schools in a rural Virginia county inform the practice of modern educators?" This review of relevant literature gave me some directions as to how to proceed to answer that question by providing a context of studies of one-room schools, past and present, and of methodological models which have been used by researchers treating them. Further insight into my purpose came from the relevant theory and models comprising the last section of the review.

Chapter Three presents a discussion of the plan for the research on which the study is based and a discussion of the naturalistic paradigm out of which its qualitative methodology operated. In it, I describe the respondents for the study and the setting.

Notes

1. William A. Link, *A Hard Country and a Lonely Place: Schooling, Society, and Reform in Rural Virginia, 1870-1920* (Chapel Hill, NC: University of North Carolina Press, 1986).

2. A.C Monahan, *The Status of Rural Education in the United States* (Washington, D.C.: U.S. Bureau of Education, Bulletin No. 8, 1913).

3. Edgar W. Knight, *Public Education in the South* (New York: Ginn and Company, 1922).

4. Cornelius J. Heatwole, *A History of Education in Virginia* (New York: Macmillan and Co., 1916).

5. Mountain Plains Library Association. "Instructions to Staff Members Prior to Beginning Research," in *Country School Legacy: Humanities on the Frontier* (Silt, CO: Mountain Plains Library Association, 1980).

6. Andrew Gulliford et al., "Work and Leisure in Country Schools in Wyoming," in *Country School Legacy: Humanities on the Frontier* (Silt, CO: Mountain Plains Library Association, 1981).

7. Jessie L. Embry, "Schoolmarms of Utah: Separate and Unequal," in *Country School Legacy: Humanities on the Frontier* (Silt. CO: Mountain Plains Library Association, 1981).

8. Phillip L. Brown, "The Young Citizens' League: Its Growth and Development in South Dakota to 1930," in *Country School Legacy: Humanities on the Frontier* (Silt CO: Mountain Plains Library Association, 1981).

9. Andrew Gulliford, *America's Country Schools* (Washington, D.C.: Preservation Press, 1984).

10. Ernest Grundy, "The Country School in Literature," in *Country School Legacy: Humanities on the Frontier* (Silt, CO: Mountain Plains Library Association, 1981).

11. Tony L. Williams. "A Salute to the West Virginia One-Room Schools," *Journal of Rural and Small Schools* 1, 2 (1986): 29-32.

12. Michael T. Tierney, "Bread on the Water: Education in an Isolated Mountain Community," *Human Services in the Rural Environment* 8, 3 (1983): 3-11.

13. Russ Rice, "The Last Class at Daniel's Creek," *Appalachia* 20, 2 (1987): 16-22.

14. Daniel Tysen Smith, *Appalachia's Last One-Room School: A Case Study in Kentucky* (doctoral dissertation, University of Kentucky, 1988).

15. Smith, *Appalachia's Last One-Room School*, 135.

16. Leslie Swanson, *Rural One-Room Schools of Mid-America* (Moline, IL: Author, 1984).

17. J.Clarine J. Boyken, *Echoes of Spring Valley* (Titonka, IA: Author, 1978).

18. Wendell Howard, "Progressing Education," *Phi Delta Kappan* 66, 10 (1985): 707-710.

19. Norman Anderson, "I Remember Springdale School," *Rural Educaation* 8, 2 (1987): 1-3.

20. Vera Gerken Kurtz, "My First Year at School, 1895," *Learning* 4, 6 (1976): 22-27.

21. Jesse Stuart, *To Teach, To Love* (New York: World Publishing Company, 1970).

22. Jesse Stuart, *The Thread That Runs So True* (New York: Scribner's, 1949).

23. Ruth Dropkin, ed. *Recollections of A One-Room Schoolhouse (An Interview With Marian Brooks)* (New York: City College Center for Open Education, 1975).

24. Mark Dewalt & Bonnie Troxell, "Case Study of an Old-Order Mennonite One-Room School (paper presented at the annual meeting of the American Educational Research Association, New Orleans, LA, 5-9 April 1988).

25. Dewalt & Troxell, "Case Study," 12.

26. Timon Covert, *Educational Achievements of One-Teacher and Larger Rural Schools* (DHEW Bulletin No. 15) (Washington, D.C.: Office of Education, 1928).

27. ———. *One-teacher Schools in the States of the Old Confederacy,* Nashville, TN: Southern Education Reporting Service, 1966).

28. Katharine Bertani, *A Program for Art in Schools.* (Brisbane, Australia: Priority Country Area Program Office Report No. 3, 1986); M.F Fogarty, *A Multiple Progress Plan for the Small School? Kelvin Grove,* (Australia: North Brisbane College, 1982).

29. R. Nash, et al., "The One-Teacher School, *British Journal of Educational Studies* 24, 1 (1976): 12-32.

30. Ivan Muse, et al., *The One-Teacher School in the 1980's* (Fort Collins, CO: National Rural Education Association, 1987).

31. Warren Hughes, *The One-Teacher School: A Disappearing Institution* (Washington, D.C.: Center for Education Statistics, Report No.7, 1986).

32. Ivan Muse, et al., "A Study of the Performance of Students from Small Country Elementary Schools When They Attend High School." (paper presented at the National Rural Education Conference, Cedar Rapids, IA, October 1985).

33. Bruce Barker, "Teachers in the Nation's Surviving One-Room Schools, *Contemporary Education* 3 (1986a): 148-50; Bruce Barker, "Where Two or Three Are Gathered Together: A Profile of One-Teacher Schools, *Texas Tech Journal of Education* 1 (1986b): 35-40; Bruce Barker et al., "One-Teacher Schools in America Today (paper presented at the 76th Annual Conference of the Rural Education Association, Olympia, WA, October 1984).

34. Bruce Barker and Ivan Muse, "One-Room Schools of Nebraska, Montana, South Dakota, California, and Wyoming," *Research in Rural Education* 3 (1986): 127-30.

35. Jack Cousins, *Rural School Communities in Colorado* (ERIC Document Reproduction Service No. ED 239 800, 1983).

36. Michael Scott, *La Prairie Country Schools: Brief History of the One-Room Schools La Prairie Township, Rock County, Wisconsin* (Rock County, WI: Rock County Historical Society, 1982).

37. Clark E. Gardener, "A Survey of Rural Schools in Montana," *Principal* 65, 1 (1984): 6-12.

38. Phil Alkire, "One-Room Schools—Still Alive and Well in South Dakota," *Small School Forum* 3, 3 (1982): 16-18.

39. Mark Kindley, "Little Schools on the Prairie Still Teach a Big Lesson," *Smithsonian* 16, 7 (1985): 118-131.

40. Alkire, "One-Room Schools."

41. Muse et al., *The One-Teacher School in the 1980's.*

42. Mark Dewalt, "One-Room Schools in the United States" (paper presented at the meeting of the Eastern Educational Research Association, Savannah, GA., February 24, 1989): 15.

43. Marilyn Kay Johnson et al., *The Big Job in the Small Schools or In a One-Teacher School, Can You Call It Mainstreaming?* (ERIC Document Reproduction Service No. 245 845, 1983).

44. Lance Blackwood, *More Like a School Family Than Just a Teacher and His/her Students. Is a One-Teacher School For You?* (Anchorage, AK: L.C.'s Manner Publications, 1982).

45. Bruce A. Miller, *Teacher Preparation for Rural Schools* (Portland, OR: Northwest Regional Educational Laboratory, 1988).

46. Judith Kleinfeld & G. Williamson McDiarmid, *Effective schooling in rural Alaska: Information for the Rural Effective Schools Project* (Fairbanks, AK: Alaska University Institute of Social, Economic and Government Research, 1983).

47. Muse, et al., *The One-Teacher School in the 1980's.*

48. Muse, et al., "Performance of Students from Small Country Elementary Schools."

49. Barker and Muse, "One-Room Schools of Nebraska, Montana, South Dakota, California, and Wyoming."

50. Jeanne Una Masson-Douglas, *Learning Environments of Small Rural Schools: A Profile of Selected One-Room Schools in Rural Communities of New England* (doctoral dissertation, University of Massachusetts, 1982).

51. Masson-Douglas, *Learning Environments of Small Rural Schools,* 2.

52. Mark Dewalt & Bonnie Troxell, "Case study."

53. Marlow Ediger, *Old-Order Amish and the Philosophy of Education* (ERIC Document Reproduction Service No. ED 261 837, 1985).

54. Marlow Ediger, *Old-Order Amish, Culture, and the Language Arts* (ERIC Document Reproduction Service No. ED 241 193, 1983).

55. Daniel Fader, James Duggins, Tom Finn & Elton McNeil, *The New Hooked on Books* (New York: Berkley Books, 1976):

56. Fader, *The New Hooked On Books,* 60.

57. Fader, *The New Hooked on Books,* 63.

58. Fader, *The New Hooked on Books,* 9.

59. Fader, *The New Hooked on Books,* 10.

60. Fader, *The New Hooked on Books,* 10.

61. Fader, *The New Hooked on Books,* 11.

62. Fader, *The New Hooked on Books,* 11.

63. Fader, *The New Hooked on Books,* 12.

64. Fader, *The New Hooked on Books,* 37.

65. William Glasser, M.D. *Control Theory in the Classroom* (New York: Harper and Row, 1986): 136-137.

66. Glasser, *Control Theory in the Classroom,* 15.

67. Glasser, *Control Theory in the Classroom,* 15.

68. Robert Slavin, *Co-operative Learning* (Washington, D.C.: National Education Association, 1982).

69. *Wikipedia Encyclopedia,* s.v. "William Glasser," http://en.wikipedia.org/wiki/Willaim Glasser.

70. Paulo Freire, and Donaldo Macedo, *Literacy: Reading the Word and the World* (South Hadley, MA: Bergin and Garvey, Publishers, 1987).

71. Glasser, *Control Theory in the Classroom.*

72. Slavin, *Co-operative Learning*.

Chapter Three
Two Respondents: A Comparison

The purpose of this study, which treats the experience of people who went to and taught in one-room schools in Buckingham County, Virginia, after 1910, has been to determine how that experience might inform the practice of modern educators. Fundamental to that purpose is the delineation of characteristics which define those schools. One of those defining characteristics in Buckingham County, as well as in the rest of Virginia and the South, was segregation. Another was that the schools were closely bound to their individual communities. That the racial and the socio-economic characters of the community would be major factors in the quality of the educational experience revealed in the interviews which are my data might be a logical expectation. However, this expectation was not borne out by my findings.

In their diversity, the respondents for my study represented wide racial and socio-economic continua. They included both African-Americans and Caucasians. They included people whose socio-economic origins were affluent middle-class, children of the older wealthy families of the County, prominent in African-American or Caucasian communities. They included people of both races whose origins were "blue-collar" lower and lower-middle class. Among them also were both African-Americans and Caucasians whose origins were impoverished lower-class.

As I analyzed the data collected from the twenty respondents, it became apparent to me that two respondents coincidentally represented both ends of each continuum, racial as well as socio-economic. They were Mr. G. Frank Harris and Dr. James M. Anderson.

The first, Mr. G. Frank Harris, age 75 at the time, was an African-American. He was born in a house which had two floors, one room on each. As a teenager, he built a small room onto the house himself because he wanted privacy. Following are excerpts from his interview done on September 9, 1989, which describe his origins and circumstances. [In these excerpts, as well as in those used throughout this chapter, "*I:*" represents the researcher/interviewer. "*H:*"represents Mr. Harris.]

H: Well, when I was growing up, we were poor as Job's turkey, but Momma was there. She'd see that your ears were clean, wash them for you, but you didn't want her to do that but once or twice. She did it hard on purpose. But you see, she was there to be sure you were kind of clean, to put out clothes the night before. . . . She would hear your lessons, too. She couldn't read, but she wanted you to go by her and hear that lesson every day. You had to read to her, or she was going to get on you. That was a little different from how it is now. The teacher came by and talked to her about you. If you misbehaved there and the teacher went so far as to whip you, you knew you would get a worse whipping at home.

I: How did you learn to read—at home or at school?

H: Both. My mother never went to school, but she could take you through the fourth grade. Well, I tell you what, back then you just read. You took the book up, and you started reading. And you could do just as well with the book upside down as not. (uproarious laughter.)

Mr. Harris taught in a one-room school for only period of several months just after his graduation from high school. He spoke in his interviews primarily as a one-room school student. He was hired as a teacher, though, to finish out the term of the regular teacher who had become ill. He said that he took the job because he needed it rather than because he wanted to start teaching immediately.

I: You made forty dollars a month during the time you taught?

H: That is what they were paying that teacher when she dropped out, so they allowed me to get the same salary . . . forty dollars. . . . I didn't ask any questions about it. It was an opportunity for me to make a few pennies, and that was good money at the time, and I had my mother and three sisters to support. I was just a boy, and so I took it and I was glad to get it. It helped a whole lot.

Mr. Harris went on to become a successful teacher and school administrator. He had attended the one-room elementary school, Glenmore, from 1922-30. He went on to the Buckingham Training School, the combined elementary and high school for backs which offered a classical curriculum including Latin, and then taught a year at Ebenezer Elementary School, a one-room school, before he went to work his way through Virginia State College. His first teaching job after college was as a vocational teacher in 1942 in Gloucester County, Virginia. He taught there for four years and then was made principal. Two years later, he was offered the principalship at Buckingham County Training School, and he "came home." He was principal there until 1954 when the Carter G. Woodson High School, a new combined elementary and high school for blacks, was opened. (Dr. Woodson, the famous black scholar who originated Black History Month and in whose name there is an institute for African-American Studies at the University of Virginia, is a Buckingham native.) He was then made principal of all grades at Carter G.Woodson. During those years he also acquired an M.A. in education. Carter G. Woodson High School is now the Buckingham County Middle School. It became a junior high school when integration took place in Buckingham in 1964, and Mr. Harris remained principal there for several years after it was integrated. In 1971, he became Director of Instruction for Buckingham where he remained until his retirement in 1980.

The second respondent is Dr. James Meade Anderson, age 58 at the time of this interview, was a Caucasian who was born in Andersonville, VA. Dr. Anderson is a descendant of Andersonville's original settlers. When Dr. Anderson was a child going to the Andersonville School, most all the big houses and farms that are now located in Andersonville were owned and lived in by Andersons or Morgans, all of whom were relatives. His two cousins, Bill and Brian Anderson, are the last remaining Andersons in that village. (They are the sons of Shield Anderson, another of my respondents.) Dr. Anderson attended the Andersonville School from 1938 to 1945, his first seven years of school. He went on through high school at Buckingham Central High School and then to the University of Richmond for his undergraduate work. He said that once he "got his bearings", he was successful at Richmond. He "came home" from Richmond to teach at and later become principal of Buckingham Central High School while Mr. Harris was principal at Carter G. Woodson.

The two men lived through the integration process together as colleagues. Later, Dr. Anderson took a master's degree and doctorate at the University of Virginia. He was then Division Superintendent in Prince Edward County from 1972 until 1990. When the Prince Edward County School Board wanted to name a proposed new middle school in his honor, he declined. He was endorsing protests from the Prince Edward County African-American community whose case was that at the time of integration, it was agreed that schools would never again be named to honor people. He appeared to be a man who stands by his principles.

The information in the following section of his interview indicates a contrasting socio-economic background compared with that of Mr. Harris. Dr. Anderson had just mentioned a bookcase in his school where library books were kept which he did not need to use. ["A:" represents Dr. Anderson.]

A: Well, most every home had a library of some kind. This was during the Second World War, remember when you had gasoline rationed, sugar rationed, and food rationed. The school was used to do the registration for the rationing initially. So there wasn't much outside entertainment. In my home, we had a pretty large library.

I: A room that was a library?

A: It was really our living room, but across the walls were shelves filled with library books. There was a lot of fiction, several encyclopedias, and so forth. So, Mrs. Thompson, [Dr. Anderson's teacher] of course, knew every student and every student's home, and she encouraged you to read the library books at home. Most of the people who used the books in the case at school were people that did not have books at home. I can remember people, adults, coming to my home during the War and saying, "I'd like to check out this book."

I: I wondered if you loaned books.

A: Yes, my mother would "check them out" for two weeks, and I can remember this one man picking up a book and saying that it was a love story, the sort of thing he didn't read. "Do you have . . . ?" and maybe he'd pick out one of Pearl Buck's books. We had all of Pearl Buck's books, and all the ones written by a local Christian author, Louise McCall. She was born and grew up in Andersonville . . . wrote a series of books. I can remember all the encyclopedias. I can remember having all the Pollyanna books. We often furnished the books for Mrs. Thompson to read to the students. She read to us just about every day in the afternoon. She may have read the Pollyanna books to us at school.

Mr. Harris and Dr. Anderson were decidedly different in both race as well as socio-economic origins and circumstances, representing two ends on each of these continua into which the twenty respondents for my study could be placed. If there were a connection between racial and socio-economic profiles and the quality of the learning experience in the one-room schools, it logically would have been revealed in the data collected from these two men, but it was not. Instead, the quality of the learning experience itself was quite similar for both men.

Dr. Anderson did not mention having experienced the effects of disparity in educational facilitation as a one-room school student, but Mr. Harris was quite open about the disparity he had experienced, especially in the years after his one-room school experience. He spoke here about the difficulty African-Americans had in getting schooling beyond the one-room school:

H: There were probably three or four school busses that served the entire black population in the county at that time, so they were limited as to where they could go because of the numerous roads and so forth in the area.

I: Were there more that served the white population?

H: Oh, yes. You see, at the time, the blacks had only one high school, and there were something like five or six white high schools scattered all around the county, so the capacity was somewhat different. . ..

I: What was the comparative percentage of the black population and the white population?

H: Uh. . . .

I: Was it equal or what?

H: Well, there were a few more whites than blacks. It was just about 40-60. . . . Now I'm guessing, you know, but it was roughly 40-60.

I: But certainly the percentage was not great enough that it justified that much difference in facilities.

H: No, indeed, no, no. (Said with a rueful but calm air . . . resignation.)

I: When you had your short experience in one-room schools, did you have a sense of centralization? Was there supervision? Did somebody come to see what was going on?

H: Well, occasionally somebody would come by. I remember that a member of the school board who lived in that immediate vicinity, in the Slate River District, came by once, once or twice.

I: To see if you were alive. . . . (both laughed). Was there equal black and white representation on the school board?

H: No blacks were on the school board.

I: And no blacks were in the central office?

H: No, no blacks in the central office, and no blacks were on the Board of Supervisors.

Later, after integration, Mr. Harris worked in the central office as Director of Instruction.

The subject turned to textbooks, which were bought by the parents. Buckingham County installed a textbook rental system only in the early 1970's:

I: And how were they chosen, do you suppose? I mean, did the state just say, now this is what we're going to use?

H: No, uh, I don't know exactly how they were selected in 1935-36, but after that certain teachers were selected from around the county to decide on books. The only difference was that the black teachers were not allowed to sit with the white teachers to select what books they wanted to use. The black teachers had to meet in one location and the white teachers in another to make that decision.

Mr. Harris' implication here was that the white teachers' group usually prevailed in the choice of textbooks, but the black group could send their input to the central office from their separate location. He commented that segregation was a more complete thing than I could imagine. He said it was like the races lived in different dimensions for all the communication there was between them. He did say, though, that there were some good relationships between races. They were just few and far between.

One of those good relationships, from an earlier era, was detailed by Dr. Anderson in the interview I conducted with him on March 29, 1990. We had been discussing the length of the school term in one-room schools:

A: I believe it was 100 days. I can't remember.

I: Starting about the first of October?

A: I believe it started in late September. I don't think it started in October. I have my report cards, and I don't think it started October first. I do have my grandfather's grade book. He taught in a one-room school, a black school, in the 1800's.

I: He was a white teacher that taught in an all black school?

A: Yes..

I: Was that fairly common?

A: In some degree. Mr. Charles White, in his history of blacks in Buckingham County, uses my grandfather's name and mentions his grade book, because he knew one of the students who was in that grade book. But in those days, in the 1870's, 80's, and 90's, teachers [I believe he meant that all teachers, African-American and Caucasian, had to take a test every year to be certified]. And on your teaching certificate, (and I have my grandfather's certificates), you had your grade on your test, your proficiency . . . like seventy percent or eighty percent. It was the percent you knew on that particular subject, like geography or history, and it was a certificate for a year. You didn't have college graduates or things like this. My grandfather rode his horse from his home approximately two or three miles and taught this one room school.

I: Where was the school that he taught in?

A: It was near the community that is now Enonville. I can't remember the name of the school; I believe it was called Mountain View School, and I know that they started in October. There was no set date to start. I know it started when all the students finished the work they were doing in the fields. And he has a note in the book in April that says, "And we got out of school early this year because it was good weather and every one had to get home for planting." And I have his inventory of the school . . . the number of desks and a table and something else that was in the school.

I: How long did he teach in that school?

A: I don't know. I would have to go look that up. It was several years. I know after that he was a made postmaster of the community. All the students, though, were black in that school.

I: Where did this test come from? Did he have to go to Richmond to take it?

A: No, I'm sure he didn't. I would think that the test was administered here in the County by the education board that was going to hire him to teach in the school. He did pass the test, because I have his certificates in sequential numbers. I know the test was administered in autumn, and you had to pass it in order to be able to teach. Now, I don't know what he was paid. I know he had to record the days he taught to put in for pay. Anyway, what I'm saying to you is that not only am I a product of a one-room school, but both my parents went to them, and my grandfather taught in one. I think it's ironic that during Reconstruction days, there were white teachers who taught in all black schools.

I: I find that notable, too. I haven't found any instance before in my reading about one-room schools where a white teacher taught in an all black school after the Civil War. It must have been done, but to know about it is wonderful.

Dr. Anderson evinced a great amount of pride in the story of his grandfather, pride that such a relationship had existed. From information in Mr. White's book, *The Hidden and the Forgotten: Contributions of Buckingham Blacks to American History*, I found that many of the teachers in black schools in the years after the Civil War were white. Many were Quaker missionaries from the North. The relationships between such teachers and their students and communities were not always good.

More blacks began to teach in black schools as the years passed (White 155-6). Apparently, starting in 1886, J. Lee Coleman simply chose to teach in a school near his home. It happened to be a black school, one among many in the County. In 1893, there were twenty-eight black teachers on the instructional staff in Buckingham County helping to staff sixty-eight schools, according to Superintendent J. C. Hayes' report to the Virginia State Superintendent of Education (159). Coleman taught at Mountain View from 1886 to 1902 (169). He took the yearly test along with all the other teachers in the County, and his relationships in that school must have been good since there are records of his teaching there for sixteen years.

Other data revealed that some disparity did exist in the length of the school term in "black" schools, whose student population was African-American, and in "white" schools, whose student population was Caucasian, but that was not a consistent disparity. If an African-American community raised funds to pay their teacher after the school board funds had been discontinued, then the term lasted longer. If the weather was especially good in a given year, then both the white and black school terms were often shortened so that the students could help with planting.

In their interviews, both Mr. Harris and another of my African-American respondents mentioned that the equipment supplied by the school board, like the woodstove and the school desks, often seemed well-used by the time it found its way to black schools. However, the equipment supplied by the school board to any one-room school was minimal. A stove, desks, a water bucket, a dipper, and a broom were standard issue for both black and white teachers (See "Instructions" from the Virginia Teacher's Register, Appendix 2). The noted difference, then, was in quality instead of quantity of equipment. Neither the quality of the equipment nor the length of the school term, though, had much effect on the quality of the educational experience in the one-room schools as related by the respondents for this study. If there were effects from the disparity on the educational experience of the respondents, it was their later educational experience which was affected, not their one-room school experience.

Dr. Anderson's description of his own one-room school which he attended at Andersonville was quite typical of all the descriptions of such schools, by both African-American and Caucasian respondents:

A: To go back to my experience at Andersonville School, there was no indoor plumbing. There were outdoor privies. If you walked into the classroom, Mrs. Thompson had her desk in the middle, and if you stood behind her desk, there was a table at which the first grade sat. There was a chalkboard along the whole side wall. Then there was a group of real small desks where the second and third grade sat, and then there were the larger desks next to the big windows where the fourth and fifth grade sat. The water cooler was against the back wall, and there was a storage closet on that wall, too. There were pegs for hats and coats, and then in the corner was a bookcase where the library books were kept.

Mr. Harris' description is of a one-room school ten years earlier than Dr. Anderson's, but they have strong similarities. He does not mention a bookcase, but he does mention in other parts of his interview lots of reading by both students and teachers. Perhaps his teacher, Mrs. Willa J. Hemmings, did not get her supplementary reading materials from the same place Dr. Anderson's teacher, Mrs. Emma Thompson, often got hers, but Mrs. Hemmings got some from somewhere, and she taught in a fairly similar building:

H: The building was a one-room structure about 20 by 24 feet. One end was on the ground and the other supported by two or three rock columns as it was on a rather steep incline. Behind the door was a shelf which held a bucket of water and a dipper which everyone used to pour water into their own tin cups. There was also a basin for those who wanted to wash their hands. Children's wraps were hung on pegs driven in around the walls. The children sat on long home-made benches that stretched about half the length of the building until 1928 or 29 when we got our first desks.

Dr. Anderson made the following comment which applies to the similarity in facilities:

A: Well, my experience in the one-room school is mind boggling to the people here in the school system at Prince Edward. When I talk to other educators, especially black educators from here in the South about it, about the woodstove, the outdoor privies, the cracks in the floor, they'll say, "We knew our people had to go through these conditions, but we never knew you people had that type of conditions go through, also." When I heard about this new theory of "cooperative learning", I said that that is how we did it in one-room schools.

Both men made startlingly similar assessments of the relative importance of the facilities to their early education. Mr. Harris says:

H: The building had little to do with the quality of instruction at that time. Good teachers are what made the big difference. At the time, neither parents nor students knew what a good school facility should be like. There was a high degree of appreciation for what we did have. The school, the land, and most of the equipment was provided by the parents. Hence, there was a strong feeling of belonging. . . . It was our school. It was a part of us and we loved it.

Dr. Anderson says something similar though at greater length.

A: Mrs. Thompson's teaching is my sharpest memory of the school. The facility itself was terrible. It was hot too near the stove, but you froze on the other side. The windows were drafty. There were cracks in the floor. There were outdoor privies; water had to be brought. She had to come and build the fire. It had to be tended. But what I'm saying is that with all the negative aspects, and you could look for many other negative aspects. . . . To modern eyes, the facilities alone were appalling. But that does not come to mind . . . none of it. What I remember, what comes to mind is not the negative things. What comes to mind is the empowerment of the teacher. What I'm saying is that education was thought of then by those parents, those students, and that teacher as being paramount. There was complete support of education and the teacher, and that brought a culmination of excellence. That far overshadows any negative memory. . . . Anything I needed in that one-room school from home, I won't say it was all provided, but they thought that was very important. There were discussions about your work. They looked at what you did at home. There was time to look at it; your education was important. We pay lip service to that today, but it's not really true. Mothers, of course, were home. I guess Mrs. Thompson was the only woman in the community who worked. Her daughter came on to the one-room school to her and was treated just like the rest of us.

While the races as well as the family origins and circumstances of these two men are quite disparate, the descriptions they give of their one-room school learning experiences are very similar. Each man attended a one-room school along with only those of his own race. Mr. Harris' family origins and circumstances are at one end of the continuum; Dr. Anderson's are at the other. Mr. Harris speaks of the ill effects of disparity he experienced in the quality of equipment in his one-room school and later the difficulties in getting high school education because of lack of transportation. Dr. Anderson does not talk in terms of ill effects of disparity; he points out the fact that the facilities were similar in the one-room schools, whether black or white.

Both men assess their early educational experience in startlingly similar ways. According to both, the facilities were not important. It is their memories of the quality of the teaching and learning in their respective schools that dominate, overshadowing their memories of the conditions. Also, the community involvement and the family support were mentioned by both as dominant recollections. What they said seemed to reflect an educational experience in their respective segregated one-room schools which was quite similar in quality. Since they can be placed at the two ends of both the racial continuum among my respondents and the socio-economic continuum, that similarity is fairly important to a sense of the ambiance of the Buckingham County one-room schools.

In Chapter Three, when the voices of these two men are "heard" among the voices of the other respondents for this study speaking on the various aspects of their educational experience in the one-room schools of Buckingham, the commonality of experience among all the respondents becomes further apparent. I have not identified those voices in the next chapter as being of any specific race, or of any particular socio-economic origin. I chose them for their eloquence or for their representative story value. Respondents are identified by race in the demographic table (See Appendix One) that denotes equal racial representation.

Mr. Frank Harris and Dr. James Anderson coincidentally represent both ends of two continua into which this study's respondents could be placed.

The educational experiences of each, though, display many similar qualities representative of all my respondents' experiences. Segregation was a defining characteristic of one-room schooling in Buckingham as it was in all of the South, but it appears not to have adversely affected the quality of one-room school learning there as it is remembered by these two respondents.

Chapter Four
Eloquent Voices

From the interviews with students and teachers of the one-room, one-teacher schools in Buckingham County came a plethora of views of the various schools and experiences. As I analyzed the written and recorded data that my research garnered, categories of commonly displayed features coalesced. My emergent protocols had provided some shape for them, and new categories as well as category titles evolved as I worked with the data.

I was continually impressed with the eloquence of these interview texts. My respondents spoke and wrote so effectively for themselves that it seemed they should be allowed to do so in this document as well. The interviews and the timed writings that extended them contained lengthy quotes addressing the commonly displayed features.

When I began thinking about how to report on the data, my primary aim was to evoke the ambiance of my respondents' one-room school experience. This chapter presents groupings of excerpted quotes as a means of evoking that ambiance. Each grouping is arranged under a heading which is an item from the category system which emerged during my analysis of the data. Each is followed by my descriptive discussion of the data it presents. In some instances, I combined quotes taken from answers to two or more protocol questions since they were subsumed under one category title. Some of the answers to the protocol question, "What is your sharpest memory of the school?" for example, encompassed material under the two category titles, "On Reading" or "About Writing." These excerpts might be thought of metaphorically as a tapestry which portrays individual scenes. The story that each tells leaves the reader with an impression of an experience which fulfilled a socially accepted idea of what education was supposed to be but did not force standardization through such mechanisms as standardized testing and state dictated curricula. Each voice tells of his or her own community school, but there are many constant elements throughout the materials.

The category titles around which I have arranged these voices are these:
A. On Schoolhouses

B. About Schooldays
C. Of Pedagogy
D. On Writing
E. About Reading
F. On Speaking
G. On Listening
H. Of "A Roomful of Teachers"
I. On the School Family
J. On Community Relationships
K. About Memorable Occasions
L. Of Disparity and Adversity
M. Of What Was "Good and Useful"

The voices of the respondents excerpted here are representative of the re-
sponses offered in each category. The descriptive discussion after each group of
excerpts under each category title targets important aspects presented in the data.
The groupings themselves, though, could be used as dramatic readings. These
voices, their own best attestation to the efficacy of their early education, provide
a substantive evocation of the culture of the one-room schools.

The voices of Mr. Harris and Dr. Anderson, presented in Chapter Three as
standing at the ends of both the racial and the socio-economic continua provided
by these twenty voices, are now placed among the rest. The voices are identified
as being either teachers or students. As each voice discusses some aspect of the
one-room school experience, the characteristics which are effective become defined. These characteristics, emerging from the context of excerpt groupings,
suggest themselves for reinvention in modern schooling.

On Schoolhouses

Mrs. Inez Kerr, Teacher

The Mourners' Valley One-room School was on Route 20 off Route 15.
Going toward Scottsville, it was about five miles up from 15. The building was
fairly well-built. It had two windows on each side. It had a small room on the
left front with hangers for coats. A long shelf on one side of that was used for
lunch boxes and so on. Since our heat came from a woodstove in the middle of
the classroom, we stored wood in the room, too. We had double seats with a
desk for each child. I only had twelve pupils, so it was comfortable for everyone.

Mrs. Ann LeSeuer, Student

The school was on what was called the Bell Road, now called Trents' Mill
Road, and Rte. 650, about 2 ½ miles from our home. It was called Belle Branch
Grade School and was moved sometime in the '30's to Dillwyn and reassembled

as space for the lower grades behind the high school. We arrived, fall, winter, and spring time, at the schoolhouse by 9:00 A.M. Our teacher rang a small hand-held bell. We lined up in front of the door and then marched into one big room. There was a cloak room for our jackets, overshoes, and such. There were two rows of desks and seats, one row on each side of the room. Each desk and seat was large enough for two students. Our enrollment was about 25, I would guess. The front center of the room was the teacher's desk. Each grade was called to the front of her desk for each subject or class at a special time during the day. She taught reading, writing, and "little arithmetic" to the first graders. Then she taught these plus history, spelling, language, and geography to the higher grades. There was a large blackboard covering one side of the wall. We were sent to that board to write words, solve problems, or whatever the teacher wanted us to do. Going to the bathroom was a short trip down back of the school where there were two outdoor toilets, one for the girls; one for the boys.

Mrs. Garnett Williams, Teacher

I taught at Gravel Hill from 1919 to 1923. It was a log cabin school with a woodblind window. That means that one of the windows had no glass, just a wooden blind. On cold days, it was cold, I tell you. Later they built a one-room with a hallway and a big room, right on that same lot. There was an entry hall, too. I walked a mile with the three kids from where I boarded to get there. Whoever got there first built a fire in that big iron stove. The parents brought wood to us.

Mr. John Spencer, Student

Our school was called Rival School and 'twas about a mile from my home-place going toward Salem Church. The school was on a hill built up to a big rock, and instead of having steps to the school, you stepped off that rock to get inside it. Down at the foot of the hill was a spring where we got the water. There were woods all around there, and we would just go out in the woods and get wood to burn in the stove. Had no janitor, so we had to do the sweeping in the school, get all the fires going, whatever. I just loved to go to the spring. You could kill more time going to the spring than. . .Human nature hasn't changed much (Hearty laughter.) The boys took turns building the fires. I'd have it one day, you the next, and so on through the week. Many's the time I've carried lightwood from home. . . .What we called lightwood you know as kindling . . . to start the fire. The school was swept at the end of the day. A lot of times that was punishment. You'd been a bad boy; you swept school.

Mrs. Christian Gooden, Student

My daddy built the original school on our property, but it burned so it was remodeled. The new one was bigger and had more windows. It was remodeled in the late '30's. It's right down there now. . . . You can take a picture of it. I started in '28 or '29 when I was about 5. I could just walk through the woods so I followed my cousin and then my brother. My brother and I ended up in the same grade though he was older because I just went. There were seven grades there, but it took me about six years to finish. I never really realized what grade I was in because nobody really made me feel like I couldn't go on. We had about 25 to 30 students.

Observations

The memories people had of the physical facilities were fairly consistent. The conditions they describe might seem to the modern reader appalling, and yet no respondent said that he or she particularly remembered being uncomfortable at school. The windows were usually big because there was no electricity to provide lighting. Schools were heated by a woodstove with wood supplied by the parents or, as in Andersonville, by people in the wood business who supplied "slab" wood, a by-product or waste produced by fence post production. Many of the schools had cracks in the floor and drafts around the windows. The facilities were, of course, no more than both students and teachers expected them to be.

If these students and teachers were uncomfortable, their discomfort did not dominate their recollections; rather it was the strong sense of belonging and vested interest everybody seemed to have had in these schools which characterized most recollections of the schoolhouses. At any rate, what so impressed me as a researcher was the genuine affection with which the respondents described their schools and the meticulousness with which they remembered them.

The School Day

Mrs. Emma Gantt Sadler, Teacher

I opened the door a little after 8:30. If it was cold, I started a fire and by this time the children were arriving. They helped to dust the desks and get things in place, plus get a few extra sticks of wood for the big stove in the middle of the room. As things warmed up, we talked—maybe about a new calf, pet dog or cat—whatever they wanted to tell about. At nine, they got in a desk, (all double), maybe with a big sister or brother, with a little sister or brother, or a friend.

Then came time for Bible reading and prayer, or a Bible story and Bible verses they had learned. Then some lessons for different groups—arithmetic, (books to guide work). Some oral; some written. The big ones would sometimes help the little ones. We would have lessons until about 10:30, then a ten minute break outside in good weather.

More lessons until 12:30, then lunch that they brought from home—ham [biscuits] and preserves biscuits, cakes, cookies, or pie. Then outside to play or inside if 'twas bad weather. Inside again at 1:10 for class work—reading, geography, history, writing and a story time. At 3:00 P.M. the school day was over. Some helped me clean the room, and then we went home.

Mr. Shield Anderson, Student

We caught the bus at my house at 8:15 to go 2 miles. It was a private bus owned by a fellow who lived in the neighborhood. When we got there, we played ball or a game with these little iron wheels I had. We ran them around with a wire to see how far we could go. Or we played baseball or "Ante-over" where everybody tried to throw the ball over the schoolhouse. Then we went in to our assigned seats. Mrs. Thompson had two rooms then, but she was the only teacher. There were two classes in each room. She assigned one room work, then went to the other. The school was heated with a woodstove in each room. The teacher built the fire, and us boys kept it going. We got the wood and put it on the back porch for the next day, so that was as far as we had to go. Frank Hedrick, you know, cut a lot of the wood for the school. We were always trying to get out of studying. Every now and then, we'd get on the wrong side of Mrs. Thompson and have to carry an apple to her. School was out at 3:00, and Uncle Harry's bus didn't come until 3:45 or so. We played until he came.

When I went, we had a well. Earlier on, water had to be brought from somebody's house. Boys would go out and dip a bucket of water to pour in the cooler. We made paper cups to drink from and paper airplanes to be bad with.

Mrs. Ruby D. Walton, Teacher

A typical day at school was planned by the teacher and a regular schedule was kept, from 9:00 A.M. to 3:00 P.M. each day. Most of us would walk to school about two to three miles. We unlocked the door, made a fire, two boys would go to the spring for fresh water. School usually opened the first week in October. I rang the bell at 9:00 A.M. The children were always on time, although they had quite a distance to walk. School was opened by reading a few verses of scripture and saying the Lord's Prayer. The roll was called, and the Health Chart checked.

The children had assigned seats, according to grades. The higher grades, 5th, 6th, and 7th would study their assigned work and do seat work pertaining to their lessons. The younger children were taught then reading, writing, and number work. After this, they would do seat work and study their lessons.

10:30—"Little recess" for 10 minutes where everybody would go outside for exercise and fresh air. Then the older children would have their classes while the younger ones were doing seatwork (math, language).

12:00—Lunch and "Big Recess." After we ate, there would be games until

12:40—Then afternoon classes would begin, more reading, listening to stories, writing, drawing, and number work for the smaller ones. For the older ones, history, geography, health. (Most of the time, health from the book would be twice a week.)

2:00—Time for "Little Recess" again. 10 minutes for play or exercise. We'd go in and finish classes. Sometimes the younger ones would stay outside with an older pupil with them.

At 3:00, the floor would be swept, erasers dusted by two girls, two boys would go out for wood for the next day. The pupils took turns for these jobs. At 3:10, we would be ready to go home. The average daily attendance would be around 12. This was a typical day at school, but on rainy days, there would be only lunch and a very short recess. We finished our lessons and went home early, and this was called the rainy day schedule.

Mrs. Christian Gooden, Student

We would get to school before the teacher did, and some of the larger boys would build the fire. The teacher would come on in and help with the fire. The boys would have gotten the wood the day before. They'd always get in the wood at the end of the day before we went home. We'd play outside until maybe 9:00. Then she'd ring the bell and we'd come in, get quiet, have devotions. Devotions were a religious song, prayer, scripture, recitation of Bible verses by the children. . . . You had to have a new one memorized pretty often, every other day or so . . . Pledge of Allegiance to the flag, and another song . . . not necessarily a religious song for the second one, sometimes a fun song she would teach us. Then there was daily inspection where she checked your teeth, your hands, your ears to see if you were clean . . . and for Mrs. Jones, you had to have a clean handkerchief.

Then the lessons would start. If I can remember correctly, arithmetic was the first for everybody. She only did one class at a time, but the others would be getting ready, or she'd have them working on something. When you came up to give your lesson, everybody heard, because they were all sitting there. It was all done orally. We even learned to count orally. Everybody stood up in a line, and we started at what they called the first head of the class, went right on down. Everybody had to count. When you could count to one hundred, you could tell the counting class good-bye. Then you could go on to adding or something else. The same way with ABC's. You had to stand up and say your ABC's. Then when you finished, you could tell the ABC class good-bye when you were ready.

Little recess was at about 10:30. We went outside for about 10 minutes, go to the bathroom, and play. If you had to go to the bathroom, you'd just got up and sneaked on out to the bathroom. Mrs. Jones didn't make you ask, but we didn't abuse it.

In from "little recess," and back to work on the lessons. A lot of emphasis was put on those morning lessons. She zeroed in on the hard ones in the morning.

Then 12:00 was big recess. That was fun time, and we'd eat lunch and go out to play. We brought lunch from home, or sometimes the teacher made soup in the morning, or she'd heat your lunch on the stove. She used to encourage you to bring anything you had at home for lunch. If you had soup left over, or beans left over, or anything, and she would set it close to the stove so it would be warm when you came to eat it. Then some things she would make. Somewhere she got some surplus materials and would make soup. Or she got dried milk or cocoa to make chocolate milk. You could bring anything, though. You weren't ashamed of bringing anything. We ate it and enjoyed it.

In the afternoon were such classes as reading, geography, hygiene. Another "little recess" at 2:00 or so, and often she read to us last thing of the day. Then at 3:00 we cleaned up and swept the room, and the boys went out for wood for the next day. The we all walked home.

Observations

What is most obvious about the descriptions of the school day is their basic similarity. Apparently, the routine day in all the one-room schools was carried out with little variation. The students' perceptions differed little from the teachers', although Shield Anderson seems to remember his toys more than he does the schedule. Features of the day which vary from those of the modern school day are several. There were daily devotions which privileged Christianity. Mrs. Dot Morgan commented during her interview that if the Koran and the Torah had been as available as the Bible, their verses would have also been read as part of devotions. That statement, though, is a surmise.

At any rate, daily devotions in the one-room school also functioned as a centering device for the attention of both student and the teacher. They constituted a ritual that signaled the start of the learning day that has since been replaced by the first bell of the day.

Another feature of the day lost in many of today's elementary schools is the recess. Two "little recesses" and one "big recess" were universal features that gave the children a chance to talk, play, and "let off steam." This feature provided a delineation between "lesson" time and social time, giving the latter an importance more explicit than generally occurs in modern schooling.

The primary different feature, then, was that the day was not measured in minutes but rather in the judgment of the professional in charge, the teacher. The one-room school teacher did not make lesson plans for fifty minute periods and stop with the bell. S/he was able to schedule specific learning times flexibly. The one-room school student did not experience compartmentalization of the day as the modern student often does. Scheduling structured in the constraints of the fifty-minute period has made schooling markedly different for both students and teachers, as later excerpts will attest.

The spiritual life of the student, teacher control of time, and the usefulness of "break" time are further addressed in the context of pedagogy.

Of Pedagogy

Mrs. Emma Thompson, Teacher

They were my happiest teaching days [Her 23 years at Andersonville School, from 1927-51]. When I first went to Buckingham to teach from Andersonville, they knew I was used to teaching several grades so I taught the overflow classes. One year, I had the overflow from the first, second, and third grades. I had about sixteen pupils, but it wasn't so good because there was so much difference in pupils [who were supposed to be on the same grade level]. When I taught single grades, it was harder for me than teaching a group of different graders because there was so much difference among the same-graders. Some of them should have been two or three grades ahead of the others; some two grades behind. But you see, I had to try to teach the same thing to them. I couldn't give them what I saw they needed like I could at Andersonville.

At Andersonville, I didn't have any discipline problems a bit. The parents were with me, you see, and that made all the difference. I believe that the thing I had the most trouble adjusting to when I went to a graded school was those bells. I was used to scheduling my own day. If I felt something needed more time, or if we were in a good discussion, why I went on and taught. When I had to quit because of a bell, it was real hard for me. Then again, in the one-room school, I didn't have just one year with the children. I got to know them and to work with them over several years. This way, I could help them on along and get to understand what they needed. If a student didn't learn what he was supposed to in a certain grade, he came back the next year and took it up again. That was not possible in a graded school. When I went to a graded school, there was so much emphasis on these failing grades, and the pupil had to repeat the whole thing, what he knew and what he didn't.

Dr. James M. Anderson, Student

Well, it was traumatic for Mrs. Thompson because she had to become part of a system that exhibited mediocrity. She had been used to arranging her own schedule and her own curriculum. She taught basic things like math and words by rote. She made flash cards, and when she showed you those cards, you were expected to give the right answer instantly. She had school so individualized, though, that if she was doing this in the second grade and you were in the fourth grade but she knew you lacked that concept, she'd turn around to you for the answer. Another thing she did was produce people with excellent penmanship. No-one in her school sat idle. You had your own tablet, and if you had some time, you brought your tablet up to her. She wrote a sentence or word containing something you had difficulty with, and you went back and practiced it. Writing was an art, and you practiced and practiced. I never remember a student questioning her. Because it was well-known that if you got in trouble at school, there would be much worse trouble at home. You knew your parents respected Mrs. Thompson. No parent ever spoke against the teacher in front of a child.

The school was small. There were usually sixteen to twenty students in five grades. She taught all the curriculum to five grades each day. But when she taught reading or did flash cards or did math beyond the memorization level, she could challenge you above or below your grade level for an answer. In the recitation, for example, of the multiplication table which you absolutely learned, she would look to a higher grade person for an answer she didn't readily get from the grade she was teaching. I think that that was a great strength. Any item that someone did not know, she could go to the students above a grade or below a grade to answer. That way, she could keep challenging you above or below your grade level. Therefore, you could either build up as a student doing your own work by shutting out what was around you, or you could go on ahead by listening to what was above while you worked. My wife says to me that she can't understand how I'm able to do two things at once. She wasn't able to understand how I could do my doctoral dissertation and work, too. But, you see, four-fifths of the time, I wasn't being taught. No, that's not true. When she (Mrs. Thompson) was reading the stories, for instance, she would ask questions and discuss with all of us at once. I suppose she asked questions on different levels. The fact that I wasn't being taught did not at all mean that I wasn't learning.

Mrs. Inez Kerr, Teacher

First we would have number work. I tried to work on whatever level I found the children. They seemed to like that because they were not pushed to follow anyone else. The children soon seemingly felt at home with me so it was not hard to work with them. We were learning together. At this time, I had no special way of teaching reading. Really, all of them could call some words, but there were not many good readers. As I recall, most of them were on a different level, so this is the way I tried to teach them. There were two very good readers, one in the seventh grade and one in the third grade. The others were given reading work to do on their levels. Each day, I tried to do things that would interest each child. I was kept busy trying to see that each child had something that interested them.

My classroom was somewhat like a home with one grown-up and her children. We tried to respect each other. This caused the students to try to please me, but most of them were anxious to learn. I did not have any discipline problems. I visited each home, so the parents knew me quite well. One day one of my little boys hit me when I spoke to him about something he was doing. . . . I cannot remember just what. I sent out and got a switch and whipped him around his legs. He told me he was going home and tell his mother. I told him to go on, that it was alright with me. His mother brought him back a little later. She told me I would have no more trouble with him, and I didn't.

Mrs. Ruth A. Jones, Teacher

I spent a lot of my own money on students. There was this thing called a Hectograph for reproducing copies. You bought gelatin at the grocery store and a special pencil for writing original copies. You had a flat pan that looked like a baking pan. After you mixed up the jelly with water and cooked it according to the recipe, you poured about a half inch in the pan. and put your original in the bottom. Then you could make copies one at a time.

Mrs. Odelle Steger, Teacher

One of the new things for teaching was an experience chart. I used to make big ones with butcher paper. I'd get the kids to tell their experiences, and I'd write them down. Then we'd try to connect them to what we were teaching. . . like if they were about science or such. Most of us took two magazines, *Instructor* and *Grade Teacher*. Then we sometimes took the *Weekly Reader*. The children loved that. Planning was the big thing. I'd do all the health on the same day or all the geography. You had to be a manager. I have my pencil sharpener right now that I installed at Johnson School. Got it from a catalogue, so I took it with me when I left. It disturbed class when you had to sharpen pencils.

Another big new teaching method was units. We had a sand table where we could make geography units and such.

Miss Estelle Wood, Teacher

We lived so close in the community. Quantified grading was so difficult for me when we started having to do it. I knew those children, and sometimes those numbers did not mean what they really could do. I had judgment as a teacher. When I had to punish children, I smacked their palms with a ruler or I made them stay in from recess and write a sentence a bunch of times. Then, of course, they were going to get punished at home, too.

Observations

There are so many notable features in this grouping. The first two excerpts juxtapose a teacher with a student. Mrs. Thompson's point about having a roomful of people in one grade who were not at all on the same level is one which is raised among today's teachers again and again: "What do you do when you have to teach all those levels in one grade?" Mrs. Thompson could handle that just fine as long as she had materials and freedom to teach each child as she judged appropriate. It was when she had to teach them all as though they were "same-graders" that she felt frustrated. That she had extended time with each child was an added strength for Mrs. Thompson. She got to know each child's capacities and weaknesses, and she had years in which to foster their strengths and treat their weaknesses.

Dr. Anderson points out the fact that his one-room school teacher, who was Mrs. Thompson, made multiple pedagogical use of all the materials and activities. She reinforced what the student had learned in earlier years and challenged him or her with what would be learned later. The previewing of the work in the grade levels above a student prepared that student for the time when s/he would be responsible for learning it; the reviewing of what s/he had learned earlier supported preparation. An established one-room school could be thought about as an ecologically sound organism as the student learned both intentionally and incidentally.

Another important point which is introduced here and echoed in the last section of this chapter is the difference between what it meant to "fail" a grade and what it means now. Students did not have to repeat the whole year's work and be stigmatized with failure. Rather, they had to complete the year's work. Then they could move on to the next year's work. This is a highly contrasting aspect of the one-room school experience with contemporary schooling, along with its converse, the fact that students who were able could move ahead if they wanted to. They could also help other students who were a bit less able, and be "co-operative learners" in a way similar to the model promoted by Glasser. Co-operative learning is demonstrated further in other sections of this chapter.

The teaching methods and aids mentioned in the section are notable since they are early versions of modern ones. An example is the Hectograph, for which I have a recipe in a 1909 teacher's plan book on file among the study's supporting materials. It was, in effect, the first ditto machine, and it seemed fairly miraculous to those teachers and students who used it. A last important point discussed in this section is Miss Estelle Wood's observation about the difficulty quantified grading presented for her. The issue of evaluation was one on which my respondents made very few comments. Apparently, the close community relationships we will see demonstrated further on in this chapter provided a context for each child's grade. Grades themselves were simply not a central preoccupation. Much more important was the whole student, his/her spiritual, moral, and physical as well as academic self.

The next grouping, "On Writing", contains data addressing specific writing pedagogies.

On Writing

Mrs. Irene Logan, Teacher

We taught handwriting from the "Locker" method books. We went right into cursive writing, no printing. Some teachers, though, taught kids to print first, and later in my teaching career, I did, too. Letters were something we taught them to write. Friendly letters; business letters. We mostly just wrote practice letters. The children did write to express themselves, though. Sometimes at the Friday presentations they would read poems or stories they had written. Some of the brighter ones wrote scripts for the dramatizations of the things we read. We did those on Friday afternoon, too, for the parents. Yes, parents often came by on Friday afternoons just to see what was going on at the school. Since I didn't have many materials, the children and I had to think up things to learn with. We always had to decide what to do next.

Mrs. Dorothy Morgan, Student

I remember Mrs. Thompson was a specialist in teaching Locker writing. Writing with Mrs. Thompson was a [sic] art. We'd practice the motions at first to music—for rhythm. My handwriting has been ruined, but it was beautiful at one time. We wrote little reports, and we wrote stories about things in our lives.

Mrs. Christian Gooden, Student

We wrote our spelling words on tablets made from old bills from my daddy's store. My momma would sew them together, and the one side had the bill on it, but the other was blank. A new tablet was something to behold. Paper was very precious. Very special ones were called "Big Five" tablets, and they were smooth paper. You were something if you had one of those, and you didn't waste any of it. You were admonished to write on both sides of the paper before you threw it away. I learned to print my ABC's first, then to write cursive. By the fifth grade, we were writing paragraphs, stories, and poems which we shared by reading aloud. It made you confident about talking. Mrs. Jones talked a lot about getting your thoughts together before you wrote, and then you wrote your paper once. You didn't waste paper.

Mrs. Ruby Walton, Teacher

Students loved to write. They would learn by copying a copy I'd give them. Sometimes we would have the Locker writing tablet, and they'd trace or copy, make circles, straight lines, or whatever the copybook would have. This would be for the older children. The beginners would draw straight lines, make circles, then put them together to form letters. Later they could form words. Larger students wrote reports to share with the class.

Mrs. Ann LeSeuer, Student

Much of the time, I expressed myself orally, but there were occasions where I had assignments in which I expressed my thoughts in writing—short stories about things I owned or things I had seen. There were tests and examinations on which I did much writing to express what I had learned.

Mrs. Mary S. Jones, Teacher

The students learned to write by identifying objects, words, phrases and putting them together to make a good sentence. They always associated words with objects.

Mrs. Agnes Carroll, Student

We had writings at school periodically. The first of the year we wrote about our summer, at Christmas we wrote, and at the end of the school year we would write another story about ourselves. My teachers encouraged us to write. Now I record my daily activities and those of my family every day in my journal. I have done this for forty years. I used to keep my journals in my school books back then as we didn't have journals or diaries. My mother still has those school books.

Mr. John Spencer, Student

At Rival we were taught to write from the old Locker copy book. We didn't learn to print. Just went right on to cursive writing. I don't remember writing to express myself much. Now we spoke to express ourselves, and reciting was a way of learning.

Observations

The respondents offer evidence of the use of writing as a tool of thought as well as a skillful art. Mrs. Carroll emphasizes the former. Others also mention writing as a tool of thought. Handwriting was considered an art. People seemed to strive for beautiful handwriting, and the "Locker" method stressed the rhythm of handwriting. Another consideration in our understanding of the teaching of both handwriting and composition in the one-room schools was the shortage of paper during so many of the years these schools existed. Much of the composition process was done orally or mentally because there was not enough paper for practice. Much of the presentation often done now on paper or computer was done orally by these students.

In both this and the next excerpt grouping, one can see that the reading and writing processes were not taught as separate disciplines. Mrs. Jones comments on the association of words with objects. Mrs. Logan relates how her students wrote scripts from what they were reading, and dramatized them as a means of comprehending. Mrs. Gooden, whose mother sewed old store bills together for tablets on which students could write, relates reading her work aloud. The two processes appear to have been taught recursively, sometimes with student produced texts.

About Reading

Mrs. Emma Gantt Sadler, Teacher

I don't know how students learned to read because I didn't know how to teach reading, but beginners learned to recognize words. These words were what we were saying written on a page. Our sentences were short but they carried a thought. If I said, "Please put some wood in the stove," then that could be written on a page in a book for reading. We'd recognize the words I had printed. There was no kindergarten or pre-school training.

Mrs. Mary S. Jones, Teacher

The students learned to read from one another. Many learned at home and were already reading when I met them. I had charts I had made called experience charts, though, and we would develop the experience from pictures or hands-on objects that we had in our possession. The student that listened to what was going on around him learned to read fastest . . . if he paid attention and was always in place and ready for the activity before him or her.

Mrs. Ann LeSeuer, Student

In our school, we used the Baby Ray primer at some time. There were pictures on the pages with words related to the pictures which fascinated me as there were babies, dogs, cats and other animals that I was familiar with. I cannot remember just how long it took me to be able to read, but I am sure it was a slow process. As I was the first child in my family, I had not seen many books. There was another girl in my grade that had older brothers and sisters, and she had been taught much from them, so she helped me a lot. However, it finally came.

Mrs. Emma Thompson, Teacher

After the first graders had their lessons, then I worked with the other kids, but they had plenty to do. They could look at library books, they had word cards, the new words for the day were always written on the board for them to see, and they had addition and subtraction cards in arithmetic. Their time was taken up. When we introduced new words, the older children would make the word cards, and they'd always teach the new words to the littler ones as soon as they learned them.

Mrs. Ruby Walton, Teacher

Students that were interested, physically fit, and ready for school learned to read quickly. It's hard to say how a student learns to read because each student is different, but if materials and instruction were introduced, they would learn to read. I used a lot of readiness materials like cards, puzzles, workbooks, and Experience Charts. At that time, you could go to the dime store up in Dillwyn and get little coloring workbooks.

Mrs. Christian Gooden, Student

I learned Baby Ray at home before I went, but I think I just had it memorized. I can remember telling stories to go along with the pictures. My cousin and my brothers had me reading pretty soon, though. Mrs. Jones read to us a lot. She read stories or parts of books to us three or four times a week, but she had you read almost every day, and you'd better read, too. My daddy and momma supplied her magazines from the store. She also read us books like the Bobbsey Twins. (Yes, I wondered why all the kids in those books and the textbooks were white. You ought to hear my son Cortez go on about that.) . . . We read out the things we wrote, too.

Reading was very important in my home. You always knew you were going to get a book for Christmas. My brother sold the *Grit*, [a mail circulated newspaper still published in Williamsport, PA.], so we got that. We got a black newspaper from Norfolk, and the Lynchburg paper. Everybody in the house read.

`We had a spelling book, and we learned every word. She called them every day and sometimes we wrote them, but more often we said them. We knew those words we spelled to read, too.

Mr. Frank Harris, Student

What I'm saying is that pupils memorized little books from following while they were read, and then you recognized those words and learned new ones. That's the way I see it, anyway. We learned to count the same way, began mathematics, and we learned the alphabet so we could stand up before the group and say ABC's. That part was just a matter of memory, who had the best memory, but after that it got to be learning. You might be able to say the alphabet but not recognize it later on paper, but that came along. Anyway, that was the method of teaching that most people had. There were others who had had some training and would do it differently. This is what most of our teachers did.

Everything that we could find a symbol for, they would identify it just that way. You'd get a picture of a tree to teach "tree", and take the kids outside to see them. [You'd put a] cup with a picture of a cup . . . in first or second grade, [That is associating "cup" with a picture of a cup]. They would write the words under the symbols. But then there were a lot of words for which there is no symbol as such . . . like courage. You'd talk about what it meant, and then tell stories of courage, of things people did that showed that concept. Could be either . . . famous people or stories of any person. Then sometimes they could be fictitious characters in their books . . . like Will and May and Baby Ray. Those were characters from the primers. They were engaged in various things. Then we used some Bible stories, like David and Goliath.

Observations

Some of the excerpts grouped around this category title are reminiscent of the pedagogy of Paulo Freire.[1] In Freire's description of his methods, "reading the word and the world" means establishing connections between learners' experiences of their world and the symbols on a page that represent that experience. The learners extend their knowledge of both the word and the world as they move back and forth between the two in a recursive fashion.

Mr. Harris, Mrs. Sadler, and Mrs. Mary S. Jones are essentially describing "reading the word and the world" in an overt way. Mr. Harris describes methods of teaching words for abstract concepts as well as words for concrete things. For an abstract word, stories embodying the concept of the word were told. These stories might have been from books or from the students' own lives.

Demonstrated in the quotes from Mrs. Sadler and Mrs. Jones are student- and teacher-produced texts. Their one-room school teaching seems to have resembled Freirian pedagogy again in joining literacy to the lives of the students. They wrote about their world and read what they wrote.

There were few "methods" talked about for teaching reading. It seems clear that students were hearing and seeing reading going on all day at school so that reading seemed a natural act to them. Oral reading was at least as important as silent reading. Oral reading was performed of both student-produced texts and commercial ones. In Chapter Three's excerpts from his interview, Dr. Anderson related that his parents supplied supplementary reading materials from home at Andersonville School. Supplementary reading materials and supplies again are spoken of here as having come from homes of students.

Also, because of the peer teaching that was a primary characteristic of the one-room school, students taught each other. Older siblings modeled reading behaviors for younger ones. Many students learned to read at home from parents or grandparents. Thus the act of reading was a "natural" act when the student came to it. For most students, it was an act associated with family, security, and love.

The Baby Ray primer was in common use, but there was not much mention of methods such as phonics. Mr. Harris speaks of vocabulary building from following the oral reading going on around a student. Mrs. Thompson's relating of the way first graders learned independently, carrying on their learning after their lessons in the morning, represents an ecological metaphor for the one-room school. The first graders functioned as part of the system, interacting with the rest of the school, learning from other students as much as or more than from the teacher.

As Mrs. Mary S. Jones says, many students learned to read from each other at home and/or at school. Reading could be characterized in these excerpts about one-room schools as a "natural act" that everyone who was a part of the community of learners naturally performed. It was not taught as a separate discipline from writing nor as a separate discipline from other content areas. It was taught along with writing as a basic tool for learning.

Speaking was an integral part of learning to read and of the whole one-room school, as is shown in the next grouping.

On Speaking

Mrs. Inez Kerr, Teacher

We had several programs during the school year, which each person took a part in. After a while, they were all anxious to do this. During the period before each program, I gave them poems to memorize. They also learned to speak in dialogues, which they enjoyed. Sometimes we wrote these to speak them. When they talked in class, we all tried to see that we spoke correctly. This was during World War II, and we were getting the *Weekly Reader* each week. They were all interested in what was going on in far away places talked about in the magazine. This helped their reading, of course, but we had long discussions about those far away places.

Mr. Frank Harris, Student

There was quite a bit of talk that went on during my learning. We were encouraged to express our thoughts on many subjects. The teacher planned it that way. One activity we had was a debate team in which we got into the pros and cons of local and national issues. One debate topic I remember was, "Resolved: The horse is more valuable on the farm than the tractor." Our point was that the horse could fertilize as it plowed and it never tamped down the earth. (Hearty laugh here.) . . . Our team conducted debates with other schools in the area before a standing-room-only crowd in the community church because the school could not accommodate the crowd.

Mr. B. D. LeSeuer, Student

Everybody was quiet while she was teaching. You worked on your lessons while the others were taught. We had lots of independence in the one-room . . . but there was always somebody to help. When the time came for you to give your lesson, now, you talked. I remember one day we had a substitute, a man from the neighborhood that I was afraid of. He asked me a question, and I sort of squeaked, "I don't know."

"Why didn't you ask?" he said, "You don't ask questions, boy, and you'll die a damned fool."

Mrs. Irene Logan, Teacher

We used speaking in the one-room schools in many ways. Correct speaking was an important aim in teaching. You wanted the kids to be able to speak well. Most lessons were given orally, and we read aloud all the time. On Fridays, we had a spelling bee, and the best spellers were left at the end because if you missed a word, you had to sit down and let the next person take your place. Spelling bees helped the kids who were hearing the words pronounced correctly.

When we were reading, we talked about what the passages meant, and the kids were encouraged to tell what they thought the passage meant. If I thought they were wrong, we looked back at the book to see. Sometimes we had some great discussions about books. Another thing we'd do would be to write questions about the stories for ourselves to answer and discuss.

Also, we had a dramatization corner, and the children loved that. We would often act out the stories as we read. The children would bring old clothes from home for the dramatization corner to use as costumes. Sometimes the brighter ones would write a script of the story; sometimes we just acted out as we read. We took some of these little things and presented them on Friday afternoons, and some of the parents would come by, or sometimes we put on a show for the community to raise money for supplies.

I'd get some of the brighter kids interested in something, and then we could get books for them on the subject. They could make a report to give to the class, and in that way, they could bring more things to the other children.

Mrs. Ruby Walton, Teacher

Speaking was a problem in the one-room school. Parents had very little education; some of them had never been to school. The children would copy their parents' speech. It took a lot of teaching and practicing to put better speech before them.

Speech was taught during language classes, at least the use of singular and plural verbs. Current events were encouraged. Once or twice during the week, each child would give an oral speech on some topic of interest. This gave them practice in talking to an audience. Pronouncing and spelling words from the "Spelling Book" helped create better speech, too.

Several times during the year, especially on holidays, a program would be given for the parents. This was helpful in providing better speech, for there would be recitations, short plays, and songs.

Observations

It is clear that speaking was an important part of the one-room school learning environment. First, lessons were taught and learned orally with recitation being an important methodology. Students were expected to shut their books and speak answers.

The teacher taught orally as a primary mode of instruction. Again, part of the reason for that was the dearth of paper. There was also great emphasis on correct and corrected speaking. The ability to be well-spoken was prized greatly. To become well-spoken was a part of the preparation for taking one's place in the community. Mrs. Walton talks about teaching usage as spoken rather than written work. The Friday afternoon presentations that were so often talked about were mostly oral presentations.

Oral reading is often talked about as a prevalent activity in one-room schools. The teacher read to the students; the students read aloud most every day. Of course, in a world that had not yet experienced the media as we know the media, the sound of live voices was much more important. In the one-room school, talk was the major activity of learning. The corollary of talk, listening, was equally important, as the next excerpt grouping demonstrates.

On Listening

Mrs. Irene B. Logan, Teacher

Students really learned to read from listening to others read. They were hearing the recitations of the older children while they were doing seatwork, so they were really prepared to go on up to another grade because they'd heard what was going on in the upper grades for all the years before. Then, too, you had families in the schools, and the older ones talked to the younger ones all the time about school and taught the younger ones about reading.

Mrs. Garnett Williams, Teacher

The children were very attentive anyway. When you spoke, they listened. They attended to each other, too, because that was good manners. That's why discipline was so good. . . . The children had known each other all their lives and cared about each other.

Mrs. Emma Gantt Sadler, Teacher

I think that the fact that lessons were oral and that they all listened all day to the lessons in all seven grades created interest. Also, it helped them remember facts. When they expressed interest in something they heard, it helped me to know what they wanted to know more about, and I would find extra things about that subject for them to do.

Mrs. Inez Kerr, Teacher

I think listening did help in their learning. Since I had a small group, my children could hear each other's lessons and, most of the time, were interested in what was going on. All of them were interested in the *Weekly Reader* so they learned from it even when I was reading or talking about it. It was wartime, and it told much about the war in their language.

Mr. Shield Anderson, Student

The more you listened, the more you learned. It was the only way to learn. . . . Still is.

Observations

Listening, then, was as valued an activity as speaking, reading, and writing. It was obviously as necessary for students to listen in order to learn as it was for them to read in order to learn. As Shield Anderson says, "It still is."

Neither the teachers nor the students told me much about any overt training in listening, but, as in reading, the students taught each other. The factor of older students knowing and exhibiting accepted school behaviors in front of younger ones important. Listening would have been one of the behaviors taught by example.

Of "A Roomful of Teachers"

Mr. Frank Harris, as Teacher

Well, when you have that number of students and that number of grade levels, you sort of have to . . . well, I sort of grouped them. It didn't matter what grade they were in for reading and mathematics.

I would stay close to their assigned textbooks unless I had some students in the grade who could go on and do some work at another level, but for the most, for a lot of the work, you could group, say, first, well, beginners and first graders together; then two and three, two and three and sometimes four together, and then five, six, and seven together. In many cases, they were sitting in close proximity to each other. . . .

When we got them [desks], for the most part, you had the taller desks in one area and the larger children could sit in those. I could work with that group for a period of time and then go to another group that was sitting in the smaller desks, and so forth. And what happened so often was that the work that was being done at the sixth grade level, well, the fourth grade student picked up a whole lot of that work, you see. . . . They picked up quite a bit. Here, again, I'm sort of crossing over a little bit from my experience as a student in a one-room class where we had fifty students in all seven grades. I learned as much from these upper grades as I did from my own class, 'cause while they were going through their work, I'd be listening and paying attention to what they were doing. We were all right there and so we paid attention to that and by the time we got to it, we had heard it before and so we went right on through it pretty good. Now that's the reason it was helpful. Now some of those students in the upper grades could sort of help these little fellows and girls down here in the lower grades. It put them to work, too, to keep everybody sort of busy, one helping the other, and sometimes here, too . . . children in the very same group could help each other a little bit, too, cause I'd assign them to work together in those groups, and it would work out fairly well.

Mrs. Ruth A. Jones, Teacher

I'd let the older girls work with the smaller ones on their letters and numbers. They could watch the smaller kids out for recess, too. They all took care of each other.

Mrs. Dot Morgan, Student

When I was four years old, Mrs. Thompson came to board with us, though she wasn't married then. (Her future husband boarded with us, too, and I was in love with him. When I grew up, I was going to marry him.) All that year, I cried to go to school because Mrs. Thompson's tales of what went on at school made it sound so really exciting. So, when I was five, they finally got tired of putting up with this carrying on, so they let me go. I was the only person in my grade from one through six. I got true individualized attention, but there were lots of things that the teacher did not have time to do for me. We all sang together. As I remember, we all did art and those things together, and you just learned a lot from the grades ahead of you. It was a strength, definitely. The lack of time to zero in on your particular grade needs was a handicap, but you got from the others what you maybe would not have gotten otherwise. At that age, you were never only with that age group. We had these double desks, and if I needed help, whoever was available would come and sit in the other half of the desk and do with me. There was always somebody to help me.

Mr. John Spencer, Student

The students really taught each other. Later, when I came back here to get a job teaching, they told me I had to teach math, and I didn't know math. I know now that that was some of the most effective teaching I ever did, because we all had to learn together. The students had to teach me and each other, like we did in the one-room. If we would, we could learn a lot from children. We have experience that they don't, but they're just as smart. I came from a family of nine children, and some of the later ones went to school to me, but I remember my older sister, who is ninety-eight and in a nursing home now, teaching me to read before I went to school. She was always my "teacher," in school and at home. She helped me along all the way.

Mr. Shield Anderson, Student

My sisters always helped me. They were so much better than I was in school, but they wanted me to be as good, too. Later on, I worked and helped them go to college. No, I didn't resent it because they had helped me, and I knew they'd help when it came time for me. I went to Lynchburg College awhile, but I wanted to work.

Observations

One of the most prevalent features among all the interviews which I conducted was peer teaching. This care for one another manifested itself in all sorts of contexts: reading, writing, speaking, listening, learning, and playing. The one-room school was dependent on the concept its members—students and teachers—as a community of teachers and learners. The teacher was the leader. Supported by a society in which adults were clearly in control of schools, the teacher was clearly the adult in charge, the primary teacher. However, everyone else was also treated as being capable of teaching as well as learning.

Everyone was an important member of the learning community. Mr. Harris spoke about the slower big boy who might be expert at making the fire and might be able to teach some of the other students about the kinds of wood that burned better and gave more heat. That student's peer teaching was valued by the school community, just as was that of the brightest academic student, an illustration of the strength of peer teaching in the one-room school setting.

Many of the teachers represented here speak about the intentional use of peer teaching. Mr. Harris speaks about teaching "sets" of grades (e.g., beginners and first graders; two through four; five through seven), and about setting up "learning groups" where older students helped younger ones. He speaks favorably of the practice of peer teaching as a reinforcement for learner-teachers. Mrs. Morgan attests to the advantages of peer teaching for her when she was the only person in her grade. Her needs were met by other students when they could not be met by the teacher. Shield Anderson, who was not particularly interested in academics, remembers his sisters as peer teachers and remembers his obligation to help them in turn when they went to college as being a natural sequence.

Mr. Spencer also talks about his sister as his "teacher," and later makes his analysis of his own best teaching. Forced to be a learner-teacher because of his lack of preparation for teaching math, he speaks of that math teaching as his best. He observes that if teachers would listen, children could tell them how they need to be taught. Many of these excerpts in all the groupings of this chapter reflect teachers listening to children in this way in one-room schools.

The next excerpt grouping is on the Buckingham County one-room schools' family-like qualities. The idea of the school as a family fostered the effectiveness of the peer teaching; peer teaching was effective because the school was thought of by all its members as a family. Whichever was first, these two ideas became inextricably entwined.

On the School Family

Mrs. Inez Kerr, Teacher

I guess because I had so few children in the school, we were like a family. It was really an enjoyable experience. I believe that the one-room school teacher felt responsible for the children. There were no principals or other teachers, so the one-room school was like home for pupil and teacher. I was very comfortable there, physically and otherwise. My children and I were like a family. They protected me, and I them. I think they loved me like they did their parents. Those years in the one-room school were some of my best teaching years.

Mrs. Ruby Walton, Teacher

There were very few discipline problems with these children. If a student disobeyed, he knew his brother or sister would tell on him at home, so that solved most problems. There was whispering and note-passing that had to be attended to, but as a rule, the school was like a family; we learned to respect each other's rights so there were no really big problems.

Mrs. Dot Morgan, Student

I want you to interview Mrs. Thompson. She was like my second mother, and she still is.

Mrs. Emma Thompson, Teacher

I lived in the community, and most of the people I've taught have kept up with me . . . do now. The interest is still there between teacher and student. They were just like my own children, and I'm interested yet in them and their children.

Mrs. Emma Gantt Sadler, Teacher

The children were always nice. They were willing to share. We'd do something I liked, then we'd do something they liked. They were so well-trained by the parents that it made school and working with them such a pleasure. There were sisters and brothers and cousins, and they were not jealous of each other. They wanted everyone to have some part or fun in what was being done. Out playing, they'd throw the ball so that the little ones could catch it, too . . . so they were a part.

Observations

From the portrayal of the family-like nature of the one-room school, one can observe that its family-like aspect provided a security for the learner which must have contributed to his or her personal growth as well as his or her growth as a learner. The one-room school was not a threatening atmosphere fraught with the specter of the stigma of failure as modern schooling can be for student and teacher alike.

Mrs. Kerr expresses the feeling of responsibility she had as a Teacher: "My children and I . . . They protected me, and I them." There was an involvement between student and teacher that was real and permanent. Mrs. Morgan and Mrs. Thompson still have a close relationship, but it is typical of the current relationships that I observed between Mrs. Thompson and her other two students, James and Shield Anderson. Fifty-five years after they went to school where she taught, Mrs. Thompson is still an important figure in their lives.

Both Mrs. Sadler and Mrs. Walton observe that the children were considerate of each other like siblings, whether they were siblings or not. The community relationships portrayed in the next section were one element which facilitated the family-like atmosphere of the school. It was as though the one-room school were a special extension of the community's family-like relationship.

On Community Relationships

Mrs. Emma Thompson, Teacher

I was a part of the community. I married here, lived here, went to church here. I knew these children, and I knew their parents. The parents and children gave me their full support so I had no discipline problems. I learned to know children during my twenty-three years at Andersonville. They weren't all alike, and their parents weren't, either. I knew them all, though, went to their homes and they to mine after I was married. They supplied the wood to heat the school, brought treats for the children, did whatever was necessary to keep the building in shape. They were with me.

Mrs. Ruby Walton, Teacher

In the community around the one-room school, people were friendly, though each family had its own work to do. The parents were interested in their school; they kept the building in fair condition, but the rest was left to the teacher. I have very fond memories of my patrons. They respected me and always welcomed me to their homes. They did their part as parents and expected me to do my part as teacher. The teacher in the community was "looked up to."

Mr. Shield Anderson, Student

Momma was very active with the school. She taught before Mrs. Thompson came, but quit when she married Daddy. Daddy left the business of the children up to Momma, but we knew he was there. She made refreshments for Halloween and Valentine's, and she brought them down to school in the afternoon. Lots of the mothers did that though. Parents were often by.

Mrs. Garnett Williams, Teacher

I taught in my own community, Gravel Hill, first, so I knew the kids pretty well. I went to church with them and all. Then when I went up to Alpha and boarded with Mrs. Garrison, I was just as much part of the community. I visited the kids often at home, had a meal, sometimes stayed overnight. The parents were responsible for the school.

Mr. B. D. LeSeuer, Student

My parents bought me books and paper, but they were not much else involved. My teachers sometimes came home with me, though, in the afternoon.

Mrs. Irene B. Logan, Teacher

The community gave me real support. The mothers didn't work, you see, and that made a difference. Their was real concern from the parents. I knew them, those folks around Ebenezer School. I boarded in the community, went to church there. I taught Sunday School, too, sometimes so that gave me another whack at them. I guess going to church with them kept education in the sight of the community. Had no discipline problems, or none that were of much amount. Parents felt responsible for kids, and they taught their kids to feel responsible for each other. Those attitudes were so important.

The parents were very interested in their children's education—much more so than now. They wanted to come to the school. They wanted to know and welcome the teacher. They wanted the teacher to visit and eat in their homes. They wanted to help the pupils at home and listen to them say what they had learned in school. The trustees who lived in the community would help with the building and grounds. The fathers would come and paint or fix what needed to be fixed, or even just come by to speak to us, especially the trustees.

Mrs. Christian Gooden, Student

My daddy gave the land and built the first school. They did what they could to help. My daddy supplied the wood, and he went and started the fires on real cold, snowy mornings. He used to haul wood down the with his horse and wagon. We owned a grocery store, and Momma supplied the school with old magazines from there. My parents gave extra books, too. Daddy did most of the repairs since he had given the building, but when they remodeled it, the whole neighborhood helped.

Observations

This group of speeches dealing with community involvement with the school displays a primary feature, a high degree of teacher involvement in the community. That involvement fostered a trust between the community and the teacher which helped to make the teacher a powerful and independent professional. Mrs. Thompson speaks of her own position in the community both inside and outside school, a position as a community member well-known to parents both as a teacher and a person.

The relationships between the teacher and the community were almost always inclusive of community life outside school. Teachers sometimes taught Sunday School, as did Mrs. Logan. Mr. Harris also mentions his teacher as a Sunday School teacher. All the teachers interviewed regarded home visits as part of their jobs; all the students mentioned home visits by teachers as among their fond memories of their one-room school experience. Many times teachers taught in the communities in which they had been born, as did Mrs. Williams. If they were not in their home communities (e.g., Mrs. Logan), then they boarded in the community with one or another of the families.

If a teacher demonstrated interest in doing a good job with the school, then community members were "with" her, as Mrs. Thompson puts it. Mrs. Logan mentions that mothers did not work, and so they could show "real concern" by their close involvement. Fathers would maintain the buildings.

The students who speak in this section, Mrs. Gooden, Shield Anderson, and B. D. LeSeuer, talk about their fathers hauling wood, their mothers making refreshments for parties, and their parents buying supplies. Mr. LeSeuer seems to remember his parents as more supportive than involved, but he does remember home visits by his teacher, Mrs. Sadler.

The community involvement portrayed here seems to have been of two kinds, the parents' support of the school and the teacher, and the teacher's willingness to participate in the community life outside school. Some of the stories of "memorable occasions" in the next section also confirm this parental involvement.

About Memorable Occasions

Mrs. Ruby Walton, Teacher

Most days were typical. We had opening exercises, called the roll, and began our day. One morning, though, during a very cold spell, there was a day that was not typical. It was scary, dangerous, and very cold. The room had gotten warm, and everything seemed all right, when "all of a sudden," a child screamed, "The schoolhouse is on fire." I looked, and around the top of the stovepipe, the wood of the ceiling was blazing. I quickly got the children outside in the cold. Then I ran back in, got the pan of water that was on the stove and slung it straight up. Two big boys brought the water bucket, and with that, we put the blaze out. The boys ran to the spring and brought more water, and we slung it until we were sure the blaze was out. The floor was wet, the fire was out, and it was really cold. So we got our coats and went home that morning. The children were scared, but they were very brave. Those big boys deserved a lot of credit. I don't know how I would have managed without them. Some of the fathers came and fixed the flue later that afternoon, and we were back in school the next day.

Mrs. Christian Gooden, Student

Every Friday afternoon, there was a program that the parents came to see. One time I remember, we had ice cream—really special. It was in a big round tub inside another tub with a layer of salt in between. We couldn't wait for that ice cream. When it was all dished, we began to eat, and people started getting the strangest looks on their faces. The salt had leaked inside to the ice cream, you see. . . .

Mrs. Garnett Williams, Teacher

We used to have box lunch socials at the school sometimes to make money for what we needed. The girls, you see, would decorate up a box or basket and put cakes or food inside. They all would be placed up at the front, and then the fellows would bid on them. The money went to the school, and a fellow would be able to eat the food with the girl who fixed it if he won the bid.

Another time . . . I was just a silly girl then myself, you know . . . Mrs. Garrison, that I boarded with, told a story about this spring pretty far into the woods. The story was that if you went there at dawn and saw the sun on the water, you'd see the face of the man you would marry. Well, some of the older pupils and I decided to try it. We got up early, met, and walked to the spring. We waited and waited, but, you know what? The sun never hit that spring because the trees were too thick. We waited quite late, and then we were hurrying back because it was after nine o'clock then. We got to the road, and saw my landlady,

Mrs. Garrison, just flying down toward us in her surrey, whipping those horses. When she saw us, she slowed down, turned the horses, and left us to walk. She was a righteous woman. Then when we got to school, there was the superintendent sitting there waiting. That was a terrible day, now.

Mr. John Spencer, Student

The parents would bring in food and things to raise money to buy supplies. We used to have fairs at school once a month or so. One of the things they did was cakewalks. Do you know what those are? Cakes the girls made were auctioned off to the highest bid, and the boys who liked them would try to win the girls' cakes. Once up at Rival, we had one of these, and we had a real pretty girl in the school. Two grown men started bidding against each other for her cake, and the one who won finally paid twenty-seven dollars for it. That was the talk of the neighborhood for a long time. In 1915, that was a lot of money to pay for a cake. It still is.

Mrs. Dot Morgan, Student

Miss Blakey, the supervisor, came to visit once, and she brought this one on herself. She was talking to us, and she told about her dog. My brother asked what the dog's name was, and Miss Blakey said that she couldn't tell him because it was a nasty word. My brother said, "Well, I'll just guess." So he started naming every dirty word he knew to guess, and Mrs. Thompson couldn't get him to stop. We were all just amazed at how many he knew, and so was Miss Blakey. Anybody who would claim a dog named "Dammit" deserved it, I guess.

Mr. B. D. LeSeuer, Student

One day when our regular teacher was out, we had a substitute, a man who lived in the community named Mr. Sharp. He did something else, but that day he was our substitute. Well, we were all scared of him, and he asked me a question I didn't know. I sort of squeaked, I guess, and he asked me again. I said, "I don't know." He said, "Why didn't you ask." I said, "I don't know," again, and he said, and I'll never forget it, "If you don't ask questions, boy, you'll die a damn fool!" He was right, you know.

Mr. Frank Harris, Student

This was strictly a farming community where the larger, older boys stayed at home to work during fair weather, but in cold weather, they all came to school. On a bad, snowy day, the regular teacher was ill so she sent a substitute who came on horseback. She thought she'd attempt to inject a little fear in the minds of these students by applying a switch to several of those older boys. One of them who was much larger and stronger that this substitute teacher would catch the switch in his hand so the teacher could not take it away until he let go. This was good fun for the students, but most frustrating for the little teacher.

Well, when the day was finally over, and the teacher was ready to go home, the teacher couldn't mount her horse. The boys stood back and watched her attempts as the horse refused to obey her commands. Finally, one boy, then another took hold of the horse and with the use of well established horse language and a strong hand, they helped the lady on the horse. Nobody laughed until she was out of sight. This teacher never substituted again.

Observations

The stories of memorable occasions recorded in this section are only a brief selection of the stories told to me with affection by my respondents as part of the lore of their lives. These memorable times stand out in the minds of the respondents because they were stressful, as in Mrs. Walton's, Mr. LeSeuer's, and Mrs. Williams' stories; because they were festive, as in Mrs. Gooden's, Mr. Spencer's, and Mrs. William's; or because they provided an undignified image of authority figures, as in Mr. Harris' and Mrs. Morgan's stories. They "fill out" the whole picture of school as a place in which the community was involved, in which students and teacher displayed care for each other, and in which each member was as valuable as any other.

Even the stories that contain negative elements, such as corporal punishment, are told with affection—which may simply mean that time ameliorates experience. Many of the stories of these memorable occasions told by the respondents were unplanned happenings. The festive occasions, which were planned happenings, like the ice cream social, and the box lunch and cakewalk auctions, involved the whole community.

As in any human undertaking, education in the one-room school had its drawbacks. Some of these excerpts do contain negative features. The next grouping displays more of the negative aspects of the one-room school era.

Of Disparity and Adversity

Mrs. Christian Gooden, Student

Sometimes I used to wonder why the white children who were my friends and who walked through my yard to school got to go to school longer than we did. Now I know that the funds for black schools were sometimes cut off earlier. If the parents couldn't pay the teacher's salary, then the school term would be shortened. Maybe the black teachers had to use their time better because it was shorter. Mrs. Jones would read extra books to us. I remember her reading The Bobbsey Twins, and they didn't have much to do with the things I knew. There weren't stories about black children, I guess. We had to make up our own about our lives.

Mr. Frank Harris, Student

We didn't know what a desk was. We sat on long benches which stretched more than half the length of the building. Everyone studied with their books in their laps. Small children's feet could not touch the floor from a sitting position. It was about the school year 1928-29 or 1929-30 when we got our first regular school desks. This was a great day. These seats were so very comfortable and provided a place to store books, a place to write, etc. They even had ink wells.

Mrs. Dot Morgan, Student

One of the reasons that the one-room schools worked was that you didn't have to go to school if you or your parents didn't want it. Many people could not get to a school because there wasn't one near, and they couldn't afford to go somewhere and board. So some people who wanted education couldn't get it. On the other hand, if you remove the segment of the population that do not want to be in school . . . if you did that now, think how different education would be. But still, education was not available to many who wanted it. Also, there is so much more that we have to teach now. Knowledge has doubled so many times since then, and the school has to do so much that the family took care of then.

Mrs. Agnes Carroll, Student

I always got perfect attendance because I looked forward to every day. I would go to school through snow and ice so bad it would cut my legs and they would bleed. We didn't have boots. One highlight was walking two miles to a local farmer's house to use his scales for our yearly weigh-in. I cherished the friends I made there, and I kept them all my life. The friendships and the fun we had made school so important in my life.

Observations

Although my interview protocols do not specifically ask respondents to talk about adversity and disparity, they do not ask respondents to talk only about good elements of one-room schools either (See Appendix II). Relatively little mention, however, was made of disparity and adversity. Mrs. Gooden and Mr. Harris both mentioned the inequities in funding and in furniture supplied by the school board to "black" and "white" schools, and both mentioned the lack of African-American history in textbooks. Mrs. Gooden said she was troubled by the lack of stories about African-American children. Neither, though, particularly indicated that these things were major devaluations of the quality of instruction in black one-room schools.

Others mention punishments which might seem severe to modern readers, but these punishments do not seem to have made much difference to their evaluation of their one-room school experience. The fact that they walked a mile or two to school in all weathers did not seem to make an appreciable difference to them either.

Mrs. Dot Morgan does bring up what seems to be a major point for consideration. That part of the school age population which did not want to come to school were not forced to do so. If their parents did not force them, they did not come. On the other hand, some children who wanted schooling could not get it because they lived too far away from a school and could not afford to board near enough to go to one.

The fact that much of the population who might have been behavior problems simply did not attend seems a notable factor in the whole ambiance of the one-room school. The parents whose children attended were parents who strongly desired education for their children, who offered support and cooperation of all kinds, who backed the teacher and the teacher's discipline. The children who attended were made aware of the value and privilege of education.

In Chapter One of this book, I quoted Marian Cramer as saying that modern educators should attend to what was "good and useful" about one-room schools. In contrast to disparity and adversity, the last excerpt grouping of this chapter is under the category title "Of What Was Good and Useful."

Of What Was Good and Useful

Dr. James M. Anderson, Student

One of the best things about the one-room schools was the fact that the growth of the student as a person was nurtured. Also, the lack of failure was a positive quality. You didn't really fail; you just took longer to learn what you should learn. . . . There was no stigma. I don't think we realized as students do today . . . that here was somebody who didn't do well in the reading lesson or in the math. I think it was that the teacher handled this. . . .You were going to learn it, whatever it was. There wasn't any question about it. You were going to repeat it, and I think she would expect you to do this at home. She not only told you to do it at home, but she told Momma and Daddy exactly what to see that you did at home. Actually, the one-room school fostered independent scholarship, too. The student was much more personally responsible for his learning. You could call it accountability. Then, the teacher made multiple use of her teaching activities since they had to serve so many grade levels. That was a strength.

Mrs. Emma Thompson, Teacher

I believe that the thing I had the most trouble adjusting to when I went to a graded school was those bells. I was used to scheduling my own day. If I felt something needed more time, or if we were in a good discussion, why I went on and taught. When I had to quit because of a bell, it was real hard for me. Then again, in the one-room school, I didn't have just one year with the children. I got to know them and to work with them over several years. This way, I could help them on along and get to understand what they needed. If a student didn't learn what he was supposed to in a certain grade, he came back the next year and took it up again. That was not possible in a graded school. When I went to a graded school, there was so much emphasis on these failing grades, and the pupil had to repeat the whole thing, what he knew and what he didn't.

Mr. John Spencer, Student

The students taught each other. I've always maintained that students learn more from each other than from the teacher. In the one-room school that was even more true. We could help each other; the larger ones could help the smaller ones. Then we could hear the lessons from the higher grades and pick up a lot from that. When we got up to that grade, we were ready to learn.

Another good thing was that the teachers knew the students and parents so well. The teachers visited in homes and understood a lot about the children from that.

Mrs. Mary S. Jones, Teacher

There was a much closer relationship of pupil to teacher, teacher to parent, and pupil to pupil. Now I don't even know the majority of "my" parents.

Mr. B. D. LeSeuer, Student

The small size made for better control, I think. The older and younger kids being together was not a bad thing. The older kids sort of showed the younger ones how to behave. Of course, the schools being so close to home . . . that was good, too. It had all kinds of benefits. You weren't scared because it was your home environment, and you didn't want to show off so much because you were so close to your parents.

Mrs. Christian Gooden, Student

I believe the teachers could really try to get students to learn, to help them get a quality education. The teacher showed interest in each child and took time for them. The teacher was in complete control. She set her own schedule, was her own boss pretty much. Her professional opinion carried in the community.

Observations

This excerpt grouping features many of these good and useful things. Dr. Anderson, in his excerpt, provides first the nurturing of personal growth. "Personal growth" is a label which could subsume many of the other things discussed in these groupings such as attention to the spiritual and moral life of the child. He then speaks of the difference in the concept of "failure": no repeating of a whole grade, and no stigma. Next he cites the exact instructions to parents as to how to help a child. Finally, he cites the fostering of independent scholarship, student responsibility, and student accountability.

Mrs. Thompson, in her excerpt, displays her experience as a teacher in control of "learning times" rather than teaching to bells. She also says it may have taken you longer than it did others to learn something, but she did not lessen any expectations of the fact that you would learn it. She also values having had time for the relationship between student and teacher to grow over several years rather than being limited to one year.

Mr. John Spencer seems to have valued peer teaching, learning readiness from exposure to higher level knowledge before having responsibility for it, and teachers knowing both students and parents from home visits. He similarly valued parents and students knowing teachers.

Small size, closeness to home, and the presence of siblings in the same classroom providing security and behavior models for the smaller child were all contained in B. D. LeSeuer's excerpt. He also seemed to think that small size and closeness to home provided more control for larger children.

Mrs. Gooden, who herself had a long career as a teacher though not in one-room schools, valued the fact that the professionalism of the teacher was highly regarded rather than denigrated. She also mentioned that the professional independence of the teacher was great.

Summary

This chapter is a metaphorical tapestry of voices portraying an educational experience that is in many respects different from modern respondents' educational experience. The school facilities portrayed are by modern standards inferior, but the attitude toward them is tolerant. The respondents express a sense of proprietary interest in their schools. Those schools represented an investment on the part of the community, an expression of love and a concern for the community's children.

All the respondents relate a consistent picture of the school day featuring devotions constituting a centering ritual to signal the start of the learning day, recesses which provided a balance to classroom behavior, and teacher control of the schedule.

The discussions of pedagogy include a teacher's observation that it was much harder for her to teach "same-graders" who were on differing levels than to teach in a multi-grade situation where she could adjust the work to the individual and make use of peer teaching. Also, students who "failed" a grade completed only what they had not done the next year rather than repeating the year. Conversely, the student who could move ahead faster was free to do so. These were important aspects emerging from the section on pedagogy. Grading, too, was discussed as being a less important part of one-room school pedagogy than of modern pedagogy.

The discussions of the Language Arts—reading, writing, speaking, and listening—portray the fact that reading was a behavior modeled all day for those who were to learn how to do it. All four of those arts were very much intertwined as modes of learning. Speaking and listening were much more important parts of the learning process since paper was scarce and the only reproduction machinery was homemade. Much of what was done was oral, and correct speech was a high priority. Handwriting was treated as a personal art. The writing process apparently was carried out mentally or orally more often than on paper.

Peer teaching, discussed in its own section, was a major strength of the one-room school. The ramifications of everyone involved being both teacher and learner, with the adult in charge being the leader, are far-reaching. The learners as teachers were reinforced in their own learning. The learners as learners were not alone in their endeavors as they each had a roomful of teachers, often relatives, who could help them learn. That learner/teacher functioned in a situation which seems to have been generally regarded as an extended family. The students and the teacher were together in a pedagogical relationship for several years as opposed to one year. They were responsible for each other in a permanent way, and the relationships that developed between them have lasted over lifetimes. The school was a special kind of family which functioned amidst the strong support of the families in the community. Parental involvement in the education of children was a very strong factor in the whole ambiance of the one-room school. The teacher was a highly respected member of the community; the school was a high priority in community life. It seems to have been a place where parents felt at ease and sure of a strong voice.

"About Memorable Occasions" relates some of the "school stories" my respondents told, but also reflects that close community involvement. In telling about these occasions that stand out in their memory, the respondents usually told about negative or festive days. "Of Disparity and Adversity" displays some of the negative features of the one-room schools. One in particular was a negative feature that also probably enhanced the efficacy of the schools, and that is the fact that compulsory attendance had a different definition from today's definition and was not enforced in any consistent way. This eliminated the segment of the school population that were not interested in gaining education, though it also removed students who were not near enough to a school to receive education.

The chapter's last section portrays "good and useful" aspects of the schools as specifically articulated by the study's respondents. Many effective defining characteristics of the schools emerge from the whole context of the excerpt groupings. This last grouping features fourteen on which succeeding discussion focuses. In Chapter Five, four of the respondents discuss some issues which they see as providing obstacles to reinventing various effective characteristics of the one-room schools.

Notes

1. Paulo Freire, *Pedagogy of the Oppressed.* Translated by Myra Bergman Ramos. (New York: Continuum Books, 1985).

Chapter Five
A Gathering of Teachers

On April 10, 1990, four of the respondents for this study met with me at the Buckingham County home of Mrs. Dot Morgan. The purpose of the meeting was to conduct a videotaped discussion of how the defining characteristics of the one-room schools in which they had educational experience could be reinvented in modern education. A videotape produced from this "Gathering" was part of the materials that supported this book. The participants were Mrs. Morgan, Dr. James Anderson, Mr. Frank Harris, and Mrs. Mary S. Jones. I selected these people as participants for this discussion because they represented the range of the study's respondents in terms of race, sex, and variety of experience as either student, teacher, or student and teacher. Also, all had had experience in modern consolidated schools as teachers or administrators in addition to their experience in one-room schools. Therefore, their discussion of the reinvention of one-room schooling characteristics in modern education could be informed by both their one-room school experience and their consolidated school experience.

This discussion did not produce magical formulas for educational change. Rather, it produced a "wider lens" with which to look at my research question: "How can the experience of people who taught in and/or went to one-room schools inform the practice of modern educators?" These four people were comparable to the classic soldiers who "won the battle but lost the war"; they felt that while their one-room school experience had reflected effective education, its features could not be reinvented. They proceeded to articulate the obstacles in the course of the discussion. They cited many effective characteristics of one-room schooling, among them: peer teaching, fostering of independent scholarship, attention to the personal growth of the child, teacher empowerment, and close parental involvement in schools. The obstacles to their reinvention, as seen by these respondents, are dimensions of modern consolidated education which, viewed from the context of their experience, are worth noting in order to provide the fullest consideration of the implications of this study.

Obstacles to Reinvention of Effective One-Room Schooling Characteristics

One of the obstacles articulated in the discussion among these four respondents was the number of state and federal controls which must be satisfied in the course of implementing education in today's public school system. Dr. Anderson put it this way:

> I don't think there's any question about it. There wasn't any structured curriculum. You didn't have the state coming in and saying this is what had to be done, or what you had to do had to be thus and so, or you had to teach this. . . . There was much greater independence. . . . Even though you had your independence in it, you worked within society, and didn't question the school, the teacher, or the education.

The respondents discussed various effects of state and federal controls. One was the record keeping that teachers must do to prove they have taught a curriculum and a textbook that are dictated from the state level. Mr. Harris commented that he knew many vocational teachers who spent so much time satisfying the requirements for report writing that their teaching was necessarily limited. Mrs. Morgan, who was a vocational teacher, said she had retired early because of, among other reasons, that need to spend too much time satisfying requirements:

> You spend so much time putting on paper something that really doesn't amount to much. It doesn't prove anything. You can't prove what somebody has learned. You can't really prove that you have taught, because the student might have it today and tomorrow he won't. And I think that the teacher who is really interested in the students is going to do the best she can with them at that point in time, and if we have to spend half of that point in time saying what we are going to do or what we have done, then we aren't getting anywhere. In the vocational subjects, especially, there was a lot of that kind of 'accountability.' (She made quotes with two sets of fingers). I think teachers should be accountable; I'm not opposed to that at all. But I think we have to define accountability, and I don't know how to do it.

Dr. Anderson interjected that the teacher was accountable to both the community and to administrators in the one-room school era, but that her word was taken when she said what she had done.

> In this society, teachers have to defend themselves. They have to fill out all these forms, all this data, to demonstrate that this work has been done. Education is on the defensive, because you've not only got to say

you've done it, your word is not taken and you've got to show on paper
that it's been done. That's what saps the time and energy.

Mrs. Jones further underlined Dr. Anderson's point by saying, "That's right.
It takes your enthusiasm away. You spend so much energy that you lose your
enthusiasm." Dr. Anderson then allowed that the paperwork has to be done in
order to get funding for the programs involved. Yet another aspect of state and
federal intervention was broached by Mrs. Morgan:

> Because of the pressures from outside the school, we are not allowed to
> talk about ethics, morals, and such, as much as were taught to us when
> we went to one-room schools. That was as much a part of our education
> as how to read and write, if not maybe more a part of it . . . and when
> we say that students feel that their education is detached from their life
> outside education . . . well, that was a part that went with them and has
> been neglected for some of them. I'm not putting any blame anywhere.
> I wouldn't know where to put it. But education is going to have to real-
> ize that we can't remove the student from his own accountability or his
> morality. . . . There are certain ethical values that can be separated from
> the religion. Plain good manners . . . respect.

Mrs. Morgan's comments address a topic that was mentioned in Chapter
Four, educating the whole child. She sees the possibility of separating such education from religion.

The final aspect of state and federal intervention discussed was cited by Dr.
Anderson in relationship to one of the one-room schools' major strengths—
multi-level classes which provided the opportunity for peer teaching. Both Mr.
Harris and Mrs. Morgan had made comments reflecting the fact that peer teaching involved transmittal of values as well as knowledge. "Upper grade students,"
Mrs. Morgan said, "did a lot of behavior modeling for lower grade students. But
they were all working out of an established society."

More of the strengths of peer teaching from the upper grades to the lower
were cited, and then I turned to Mrs. Jones and asked what she would do if her
school were to reorganize and give her a group made up of grades four through
seven for whom she would have responsibility until all were graduated:

> Oh, to me that would be sort of ideal, the way you're speaking, because
> the first thing I'd do would be find out where they are in their work,
> and then I'd have various activities for all the levels. Then I would
> know if I had somebody in the seventh grade that really was a little be-
> low, and they needed to be doing work with the fifth. All I'd have to do
> is sort of shift. We do have problems today in that we have students
> who are in the seventh grade, but they can't read on a seventh grade
> level, and I have to bring in materials for them to reach a level so that I
> can do what they need for all of them. . . . I would work it so they could

help each other and to me it would be ideal. I've always called my one-room situation ideal, because if I had any problems, all I had to do . . . well, if I had a sixth grader and the fourth grader needed help, all I had to do was shift them there, and they could work as a team together, and there wouldn't be any problem at all. . . . In a one-room school, you had all kinds of materials, all levels, and you could shift them and not make anyone feel bad. And students are still willing to help one another, though it's not as easy. They don't mind it for awhile, though.

When Mrs. Jones finished talking, Dr. Anderson interjected:

Let me say one thing. You've given her a hypothetical situation that she could work with, but let me tell you that as soon as that report went in to the state, that she was teaching fourth, fifth, sixth, and seventh grades, you would have a computerized printout come right back with asterisks all over it on accreditation standards, and all sorts of reports would be demanded as justification for why that's organized in that fashion. And you would spend more time dealing with paperwork and forms and justification to support, so that any concept of what you are doing for the kids would get lost.

The discussion characterizes state and federal demands as limiting the teachers' independence and academic freedom through encroachment on teacher (and administrator) time and energy. In contrast, the one-room school teacher was empowered by his or her support system, the "web" of the community society around the one-room school. Federal and state funds and controls were not very important to one-room schools.

The degeneration of the community as a support system was another subject discussed by these four respondents. Dr. Anderson observed:

We're also dealing with a very mobile population. In fact, almost 30% are in and out of school, changing throughout the year. Very seldom, in a one-room school, did that happen. When a kid finished a one-room school, chances were highly likely that student had been in that one-room school all the way through. In this day and time, very few students ever go to the same school all the way through. . . . One of the difficulties today is the massive communications, the massive mobility of people, and the general change in society.

Various respondents echoed his statements with examples of community damage from population mobility. They agreed that population mobility is also connected to the failure of the family. Formerly, families took responsibility for much of children's moral and spiritual education. In a one-room school, the teacher was empowered to deal with the whole life of the child, but the teacher was working with the support of a community of stable families. The teacher was also invested and involved in that community, a known, trusted member. Schools have inherited many of the former duties of the family such as teaching good manners, but they are prohibited by federal and state imposed constraints from addressing issues such as the spiritual life of the child.

The next subject of this discussion was modern teachers' involvement in the duties of their positions and in the life of the community. Mrs. Jones spoke of home visitation:

> . . . In the community school the teacher knew the homes and went into the homes. And part of my teaching career was spent visiting the homes of the students I expected to have in class the next year, and that means a lot to a teacher. . . . I felt I needed to do that. And I still would, even in our complex society of today I still feel the need to do it, but I would have a fear of doing it, and that's sad to say. . . . You're not welcome. Our communities do not exist today as they used to. . . . We don't know the parents.
>
> Those parents that you really need to see, you don't see. They don't come. You see the parents of the children who are doing well. . . . You go to PTA, and you look around. . . . You say, 'We're having a little teachers' meeting. Where are the parents?'

Mr. Harris pointed out that many parents do not feel comfortable coming to school because they feel they have to dress up and make arrangements to visit, i.e., since it is not "their" school. These respondents felt that the relationship between parents and school has changed immensely. However, they also felt that teachers should act as role models for students; the implication was that sometimes modern teachers do not do so. Mr. Harris said that he had interviewed people for positions as teachers in Buckingham County who were not suitably dressed:

> When I was in a position to interview people for teaching jobs, and one came in for an interview with his hair all sorts of ways and clothes hanging any old way, why I would not give that person a full interview. I did not think he would suit the classroom.

When they were discussing the teaching of such things as good manners and respect, Mrs. Morgan said:

> And I think one of the best ways of teaching is by example as a model. For the student, it's not what you say as much as it is what you do. I think a teacher can get those things across by being a proper role model.

Dr. Anderson reinforced her statement by saying:

When I'm talking role models, I'm not thinking so much about appearance as I am about integrity, honesty, trustworthiness with the students, and responsibility with the students. You don't fool those students; they know. And I'm saying that being the proper role model, making sure that you demonstrate those values I think goes a lot further than just saying them, teaching them.

Mrs. Jones commented further that a real teacher has to love students:

Some of my students say, 'Mrs. Jones, you seem happy all the time. You feel good, you come to school all the time, very seldom miss. . . .' And I say, 'That's because I enjoy what I'm doing. I love you, I love all of you. That's why I'm here.' I think the feeling you have toward the students and what you are doing is important. To teach children in this day and time, with these children, you've got to love them, I tell you.

On the other hand, the respondents agreed that being a role model and expressing one's love of children is difficult when teachers feel as constrained as they often do in today's schools. In response to my asking whether they felt "vested interest" or "ownership" in the school system as it now exists, Dr. Anderson laughed and said he felt "put on the spot" by the word "ownership." As division superintendent in the same district for eighteen years, he felt "ownership" when he did things like ordering reroofing for buildings he had ordered the first roofs for, but: "I think that if I were a classroom teacher, I would feel I had no ownership and wasn't a part of it."

Mrs. Morgan said:

Well, see, I always felt I was [a 'part of it', as Dr. Anderson had just said]. I always felt like that little home ec. cottage down there belonged to me. And if I hadn't felt that way, I wouldn't have wanted to sweep the floor . . . and make the money to put the walk in front of it and buy the sink. If I hadn't felt that way, I don't think I could have put my heart into it and progressed. I didn't feel like it belonged to me so I could order people around and that sort of thing, but I felt a real vested interest in it. And when you get to the point that you can't feel like that, I don't think you can do your best teaching . . . and how can you teach students that they'll have to have it [a vested interest] in whatever they go out in life to do if they're going to be happy and successful in anything, if you can't feel vested interest in what you do?

The last issue discussed in this "gathering of teachers" was student accountability, and it was directly related to teachers' loss of empowerment. These respondents felt that the lack of student accountability, that is, students being responsible for their learning and learning behavior, is partly a result of lessened family involvement and support.

Other causes they cited, though, were that loss of "vested interest" on the part of teachers and the shift to "child-centered" educational models in the 1930's. (The term "child-centered" has reference to the educational philosophies of John Dewey. Those philosophies which gave rise to "child-centered" teaching models were first published in 1902 as a pamphlet, *The Child and the Curriculum.)*[1]

Relative to that shift from "learning-centered" to "child-centered" educational models, Mr. Harris said that he remembers being aware of the difference while he was still in school. In his and Dr. Anderson's analysis, that shift from "learning centered" to "child centered" teaching models was a turning point in education in Virginia, at least as they know about it. The shift became a problem, as both these men saw it, because the "child-centered" models were misunderstood by most teachers as well as local administrators, and that misunderstanding was not corrected by in-service training. According to them, "child-centered" became synonymous with "laissez-faire" to the detriment of all concerned.

The two respondents spoke of this faulty implementation. Mr. Harris said:

The teachers . . . had not been trained for this [use of 'child-centered learning' as a teaching model]. They changed methods without having adequate training. . . . And in a lot of cases, when the child made their [sic] own choices, it might have been all right, but the teacher didn't know how to use their choices to promote education, educational growth.

According to Mr. Harris, many teachers and administrators of the '30's thought the term "child-centered curriculum" meant an obligation to amuse children by doing whatever they wanted. Dr. Anderson picked up that thought and said:

The state fostered a "laissez-faire" philosophical view of education. . . . See, what you've done with that is, you then become a reflection as a teacher. And this is when teachers do not feel comfortable at all.

In the view of these respondents, the faulty implementation of that model was a strong element in lessening the strength of the idea that students are responsible and accountable for their education. Rather, in the judgment of these respondents, the model's faulty implementation fostered the idea on the part of students that they did not have much obligation to engage, to exert themselves to learn.

Summary

"A Gathering of Teachers," the discussion among four respondents for this study, was an occasion during which several issues were articulated as obstacles to the reinvention of the effective characteristics of one-room schooling. These obstacles included state and federal interventions in the form of state and federal controls that place constraints on local independent control. They also included the massive population mobility and change in the family structure which has contributed to the degeneration of family and community structures so vital to the support of the one-room schools. Another obstacle involved was the reduced teacher visibility as part of community life and as a role model for students.

The respondents agreed, though, that teacher constraint by federal and state controls contributes to reduced teacher involvement and interest. The limited empowerment of teachers was linked to reduced student accountability. This diminished feeling of obligation to exert on the part of students was regarded by the respondents as an obstacle also to reinvention of effective one-room school characteristics in modern education.

Although the tenor of the discussion was pessimistic, the discussion produced in the "A Gathering of Teachers" carries implications for modern schooling. Those implications, as well others produced by this study, will be discussed in Chapter Six.

Notes

1. John Dewey, "The child and the curriculum" in *John Dewey On Education: Selected Writings,* ed. Reginald D. Archambault (Chicago: University of Chicago Press, 1964).

Chapter Six
Conclusions and Implications

This study has been pursued in accordance with the qualitative inquiry paradigm; therefore, its conclusions are idiographic rather than nomothetic in nature. Out of the data gathered from the twenty respondents for the study, a number of characteristics have emerged. Some of these can fairly be called defining characteristics of the common experience of these twenty people, the experience of education in one-room schools located in Buckingham County, Virginia, during the decades after 1910.

My research question was, "How can the experience of people who taught in and/or went to one-room schools inform the practice of modern educators?" Fundamental to my purpose of answering that question was the need to delineate defining characteristics of one-room schools.

Segregation as a Defining Characteristic

One defining characteristic in the one-room schools of Buckingham was segregation. Though segregation was a negative characteristic, it was one that apparently did not make an appreciable difference in the quality of the learning/teaching experiences offered in those schools. It made a difference in the length of the school term in some areas of the County and in the quality of the equipment issued from the school board office, but the learning and teaching that went on in the one-room schools attended by my respondents was not widely disparate whether those respondents were African-American or Caucasian.

One of my African-American respondents who preferred to remain unidentified in this instance said to me that it may have been a mistake to put young African-American students with Caucasian teachers because African-American children cannot fully respond to Caucasian teachers. The person was speaking from the vantage point of teaching experience in both integrated and segregated schools. Paulo Freire writes in *Pedagogy of the Oppressed* about the resistance

84   Chapter Six

of people in the non-dominant culture to the dominant culture's attempts to
teach them.

> No pedagogy which is truly liberating can remain distant from the oppressed by
> treating them as unfortunates and by presenting for their emulation models
> from among the oppressors. The oppressed must be their own examples in the
> struggle for their redemption.[1]

Could it be that an element in the continuing prevalent underachievement
among minority students is the lack of early educational nurturing by adults to
whom they can fully respond? Could it be that a stronger cultural identity
formed by such early nurturing would foster the positive self-image minority
students often seem to lack? I am reminded of *The Way It Spozed To Be* when
the white coach tells the author: "Listen, Jim, I always like to get in a word with
the new men teachers. Like to help them start out right. The women, it's different. These ladies, especially these old colored ones, they have some kind of hold
on the kids we don't."[2]

The one certain observation I can make on the subject is that secure self-
image appeared to be a character trait among all of my respondents.

Some Positive Defining Characteristics

The excerpts assembled under the category headings in Chapter Four reveal
other characteristics of one-room schooling, many of which were, in contrast to
segregation, valuable. Among them are the affection and the sense of personal as
well as community investment expressed when the respondents spoke of their
schools. A major complaint of modern teachers and administrators is the lack of
parental involvement in the education of children. That lack may be partially at-
tributable to the state of the family as institution in modern American society.
This research also suggests that another element in it is the reduction of vested
interest parents feel in schools which are large, relatively far away from home,
and are "public property." The sense of schools as a manifestation of love and a
concern on the part of a specific community for its children appears to be gone.
Instead, schools tend to, as expressed by these respondents, be regarded as institutions whose measures all too often predicate children's failure rather than personal growth.

In the one-room schools, parents felt more free to visit than parents do in
today's schools. While today's parents have less time and energy for participation because of many other reasons (i.e., single parenting, both parents working),
decreased parental involvement may be partly due to lessened comfort in visit-
ing schools.

The "trappings" of an establishment institution with all the dignity and authority of the state and federal governments supporting it are sometimes hard for
any parent to deal with, even a parent who is part of that system. Perhaps parents
and students could be made to feel that school is more connected to their "real"

lives rather than feeling that life "inside" school is separate from their lives "outside" school. Efforts to open schools to the community would facilitate that goal. Allowing parents to visit without having to go first to the principal's office or to give the teacher prior notice might help, as impractical as that currently sounds.

Concomitant with the diminishment of parental involvement is the changing nature of the American family. The families in Buckingham County are no different from those in the rest of America. Many families no longer take responsibility for the moral and spiritual education of their children. More and more of that responsibility, then, devolves to schools and other social institutions. Yet, the public schools' ability to fulfill that responsibility is constrained in various ways. An example would be the prohibition of the use of religious music unless it is couched in an historical, non-religious context. Where are the spiritual and moral selves of children to be nurtured if schools cannot or will not so much as demonstrate spiritual aspects of learning, and if their families fail in that nurturing? Spiritual training can certainly be multicultural and ecumenical.

This study suggests that it might be profitable for modern educators to consider returning to spiritual or moral readings and songs as centering devices to signal the start of the learning day. There are many songs and readings that do not promulgate religion. These might be used with some of the effectiveness that daily devotions had in the one-room school.

The one-room school as a community institution took the personal growth of the whole child as its responsibility with the full support and knowledge of the community surrounding it. An aspect of the one-room schools as portrayed by the respondents for this study, making possible the fostering of the child's personal growth, was teacher empowerment. Teachers, once they became active members of the community, were in charge of the school and all that school did. They scheduled both learning time and social time, giving balance of the two importance. They diagnosed each student's ability and learning level, and adjusted work and materials accordingly. Teachers specifically instructed the parents in what they could do to help their child. They defined (or refused to define) failure, and they evaluated each student in terms of his or her ability and effort based on a full knowledge of that student's life in the larger context of the community.

Theirs was an effective teacher accountability, one premised on direct responsibility to the community to educate citizens capable of functioning in it and to educate the community to receive those citizens. Today's education has lost much of that direct accountability because schools have become so much bigger, so much farther removed from any one community, and so much more subject to state and federal controls. Such direct accountability is seldom feasible in large, consolidated public schools. This study suggests that schools may have grown too big.

A characteristic that probably made one-room schools more workable was that compulsory schooling was not enforced. This meant the one-room school population comprised only people who could get to a school, and many who wanted education could not get to one. Consolidated schools supported by a bus system have enabled more people to get to school.

However, the lack of enforced compulsory schooling also meant that the population in one-room schools was usually made up of people who wanted to be there. That is certainly a defining characteristic of the one-room situation which enabled quality instruction, one whose reinvention in modern education appears unlikely given the present laws which force school attendance now through the child's eighteenth year or graduation.

The population of students and teachers, at least within the boundaries of this study, was a population who wanted to be in school and who understood the value of education. This factor facilitated close involvement, family-like involvement, among the whole learning community in one-room schools. Students taught each other and felt responsible for each other's success. The relationships formed in one-room schools among my respondents were lifetime relationships, between students as well as between teachers and students. It is difficult for modern teachers and students to understand the idea of school as family as it is portrayed in this study. Rather, school is often seen as the aggressor. Instead of close relationships between students and teachers, teachers must refer students to other personnel or agencies if they discern problems in students' lives. Close teacher-student relationships are, at best, often thought to impugn the objectivity of the teacher's evaluation.

Because of the fact that so much of the child's education which used to be the venue of the family has devolved onto the school system, the discouragement of family-like relationships between student and teacher can leave some students without a support system. It is not within the compass of this study to judge whether such discouragement is right or wrong. Perhaps close teacher-student relationships are no longer possible; the respondents who took part in the "Gathering of Teachers" seemed to feel they were not. Certainly the modern public school system does little to foster such relationships.

An important element in these family-like relationships was the fact that teachers were with students for a period of time extending beyond one year, sometimes far beyond one year. Just as there was a different sense of time in the learning day, so there was a different sense of time in the learning relationship. If a student did not learn something today, there was always tomorrow. A student's failure to learn specific information in a limited time period did not mean that the student was a "failure." It simply meant that student needed more time. Translating this premise to higher education, I recently had an experience with a graduate student returning to complete his master's. I had taught this student in undergraduate school as well. This is a quote from the e-mail he sent me.

> I sincerely appreciate you taking the time and the effort to help me out with everything. You've always been a significant, nurturing figure in my education at Buffalo State. The example and model you set for future teachers is invaluable; kindness and authenticity in character go a long way in making students feel special. I'm grateful that I can drop you an e-mail asking for help 15 years

after taking my first class with you, and that I can receive the same warmth and support that I did when I was 20. Thank you. Mike.

Perhaps modern schools could be reorganized so that the teacher-student relationship could be extended. A way of doing that would be to set up multi-grade classrooms that were longer-term. A teacher could have the same multi-grade class for a number of years. In recent years, around 2000, elementary and middle schools in some parts of the United Stated started a variety of programs that acted on this ides in limited fashion. Called "looping" or "blending", the practice has generally involved teachers keeping students for two years, say third and fourth grade.[3] The one-room school relationship model, though, kept the teacher and student together for as many as eight years.

One result of longer exposure might be more fully developed relationships among students and teachers. Another might be more continuity in each child's learning experience. Mrs. Jones' response, as recorded in the "Gathering of Teachers" in Chapter Five, to the suggestion of reorganizing her existing school was heartening. The suggestion of giving her a classroom that resembled a one-room school in that it would be multi-level and provide opportunities for non-stigmatizing adjustments to student needs elicited an enthusiastic response.

Clearly, one-room schools were not a place where grades as such were as vitally important as they are today. Reorganization in order to structure such a multi-level situation could provide the opportunity to redefine the term "failure" as it exists in modern schooling. It could provide an impetus for decreasing the present-day emphasis on grades A modern classroom situation could exist where students could move at their own pace instead of against time constraints. Then the "failure" label with the resulting syndrome which all too often accompanies it might not be so prevalent. Possibly the necessity could be removed for students to repeat a whole year (which includes what they do know as well as what they don't, all the while bearing the label of "failure"). Faster students might be able to move on, to enrich their learning with supplementary materials and experiences, and/or to reinforce their learning by teaching younger or slower students. Teachers and students might be able to build relationships more akin to mentorships if students did more than just pass through one teacher's room on their way to another's the following year. Students might be able to build deeper relationships with each other. This study demonstrates and incidentally reinforces what others such as Fader[4] have said: peer teaching was a major strength of one-room schools.

Mrs. Jones' belief—that learning teams featuring peer teaching as it was practiced in one-room schools would still prove beneficial—is provocative. Learning teams of the kind she cites bear likenesses to those models portrayed in both Fader and Glasser.[5] They also, however, bear a salient difference. Glasser and Fader both advocate learning teams in a same-grade classroom. Their ideas involve building teams comprised of same-graders with differing ability levels.

Learning teams in a multi-level classroom comprised of differing age, grade, and/or ability levels offer at least two advantages over Fader's and

Glasser's learning team models. One advantage is that older students can teach younger students not only academics but also supporting behaviors. For example, reading in the one-room schoolroom, as it is pictured in Chapter Four, was a "natural act" since older students were performing it as younger students watched them. Another advantage is that younger students could acquire what might be called "learning readiness." They could be exposed to higher level work before the time at which they are responsible for learning it.

As well, multi-level learning teams could offer all the other advantages of peer teaching. As Daniel Fader says of the multi-level learning teams he discusses in *Hooked on Books*, "No child was ever lost." Every learner had access to tutors, and could have such access today in a long-term, multi-level class. In one-room schools, the peer teacher probably profited as much from the experience as the person being taught. Teaching demands synthesis from the teacher. It reviews the teacher's knowledge, and it makes him or her process that knowledge in order to present it. Glasser and Fader both display awareness of the value of one student teaching another. Perhaps multi-level, long-term peer teaching could enlarge that value.

The implications of all learners thinking of themselves as teachers as well as learners are extensive. Teachers are in control of their subject matter; they are authorities on their subject matter. Teachers are responsible for their own learning. Are these not the very qualities desired in students?

One of the characteristics that Dr. Anderson and Mr. Harris both mentioned in talking about their one-room school experience was the fostering of independent scholarship. The fact that adult teacher time was limited made independence and peer teaching necessary. People who can think of themselves as both teachers and learners must be independent scholars. If they are going to teach, they must be able to learn for themselves, listen effectively, and process what they learn. Because they must teach others, they are both responsible and accountable for what they learn. In short, they must be competent students.

Summary

Numerous defining characteristics of the one-room schools emerged from data provided by the twenty respondents interviewed for this study. Of those defining characteristics, five emerged as possibly transferable and warranting consideration for reinvention in modern education:

1. Close parental involvement; opening schools to the community by removing formality from parental visits.

2. Renewed attention to the spiritual and moral lives of children; returning to daily use of spiritual and moral readings and songs not promulgating religion as centering devices to signal the start of the learning day.

3. Extended time for development of the student-teacher relationship; reorganizing schools to provide longer-term, multi-level classroom communities.

4. A different, less stigmatizing, definition of "failure"; reorganizing to provide longer-term, multi-level classroom communities where students would not have to repeat what they knew, but rather would learn what they did not know to pass a given grade level.

5. Peer teaching; reorganizing to provide long-term, multi-level classroom communities since such classrooms could use multi-level learning teams with all their advantages.

In Chapter Five, I have analyzed the transcript of the discussion among four of my respondents. The people involved in that discussion, all of whom had lifetime careers as educators, widened the considerations of this study's implications by their very pessimism in considering the possibility of reinvention. Perhaps their version of what they saw as the progressive degeneration of schooling in Virginia is accurate; perhaps not. The mistakes in implementing the "child-centered learning" model derived from John Dewey's *The Child and the Curriculum*[6] are only one explanation for the origin of many of today's students' unwillingness to exert themselves in their own learning, observed and recorded by many of today's educators as well.

Such pessimism is saddening from teachers such as these who have been involved with education and students all of their lives. Yet such pessimism is what one commonly hears in almost any teachers' lounge. It provides its own obstacle to positive change in education. Ann Berthoff implies this when she says: "We do not need new information. We need to think about the information we have."[7]

Reinvention of effective defining one-room school characteristics drawing on this idiographic study is possible. It would mean provision for reorganization by state and federal controlling agencies but no high expenditure of funds. For many teachers, it would also mean making an old teaching style new, which would be a revolutionary act for them. Students and teachers, though, might again become able to recall schooling with affection.

Suggestions for Further Research

Several directions for further research are possible. Three areas in particular are suggested by these preceding conclusions and implications. First, the idea of reorganizing schools to provide long-term, multi-grade learning communities could be treated experimentally or by case study if such communities could be set up. Secondly, learning teams encompassing the variables of multiple grade levels, multiple ages, longer terms, and multiple ability levels could be compared with those providing only multiple ability levels, and thirdly, the proposition of teacher retraining for teaching in multi-grade, long-term learning communities would require a theoretical model from which it could be implemented.

Public schooling in this country has been steadily declining on a national level since I did the research for this book in 1989. I have taught since then in New York state at SUNY College at Buffalo where I have prepared many teachers for the classrooms of New York as well as for those of other places in the country. I know that the teachers I have helped to send out into the system have fared pretty well, for I am in touch with many of them. Some of them, though, have quit teaching because they could not deal with the politics involved in public education. Those who have kept on are heroic in their dedication. Many of them are superb teachers. We can only hope that these can prevail in doing what they know is right.

Notes

1. Paulo Freire, *Pedagogy of the Oppressed,* translated by Myra Bergman Ramos (New York: Continuum Books, 1985), 39.

2. James Herndon, *The Way It Spozed to Be* (New York: Simon and Schuster, 1968), 13-14.

3. www.openeducation.net/. . ./looping-in-education-time-to-make-it-a-fundamental-practice/

4. Daniel Fader, James Duggins, Tom Finn, and Elton McNeil, *The New Hooked on Books* (New York: Berkley Books, 1976).

5. William Glasser, *Control Theory in the Classroom.* (New York: Harper and Row, 1986).

6. John Dewey, "The Child and the Curriculum," in *John Dewey On Education: Selected Writings,* ed. Reginald D. Archambault (Chicago: University of Chicago Press, 1964).

7. Ann Berthoff, "The Teacher as Researcher," in *Reclaiming the Classroom: Teacher Research as an Agency for Change,* ed. Dixie Goswami & Peter R. Stillman (Portsmouth, NH: Heinemann-Boynton-Cook, 1987), 30.

Appendix I
Demographic Table

Name	Sex	Race
Students		
Allen, Mary L.	F	Caucasian
Anderson, James .	M	Caucasian
Anderson, Shield	M	Caucasian
Carroll, Agnes	F	Caucasian
Gooden, Christian	F	African American
Harris, G. Frank *	M	African American
LeSeuer, Ann	F	Caucasian
LeSeuer, B. D.	M	Caucasian
Morgan, Dorothy A.	F	Caucasian
Spencer, John C.	M	Caucasian
Teachers		
Jones, Mary S.	F	African American
Jones, Ruth A.	F	Caucasian
Kerr, Inez	F	African American
Logan, Irene B.	F	African American
Sadler, Emma Gantt	F	Caucasian
Steger, Odelle L.	F	Caucasian
Thompson, Emma	F	Caucasian
Walton, Ruby D.	F	Caucasian
Williams, Garnett	F	Caucasian
Wood, Estelle	F	Caucasian

*Mr. Harris also spoke as a teacher

Appendix II
Interview Protocols

An Interview Protocol for Teachers

1. Describe the physical setting of your one-room school.

2. Describe a typical day in your one-room school.

3. Describe a day that was not typical.

4. What is your most striking memory of the school?

5. How did students learn to write?

6. How was speaking used in your one-room school?

7. What training did students get in listening?

8. Did listening figure in their learning?

9. What sort of student learned to read most easily?

10. What defined cheating?

11. Did you have discipline problems?

12. How did students learn to read?

13. Were you in close touch with an administrator?

14. Were you physically comfortable at school?

15. Can you talk about your relationship with the community around the school?

16. What five or six words would you use to characterize your experience?

17. What do you remember learning while you taught in your one-room school?

18. What characteristics of one-room schooling do you think modern educators could profit from using?

19. Did you continue to be a teacher? What further teaching experience did you have? Would you compare your one-room school experience with your other teaching experience in at least three ways?

20. How did you deal with a problem student you remember, either one that you managed to change or one that you did not manage to change?

21. How did you manage to teach so many grade levels at once?

An Interview Protocol for Students

1. When and where did you attend a one-room school?

2. Describe a typical day at your school.

3. Describe a day that you remember which was not typical.

4. Who was your teacher?

5. What is your sharpest memory of the school?

6. How do you remember your parents in relationship to the school?

7. When and how did you learn to read?

8. When and how did you learn to write?

9. Did you write to express yourself at school?

10. Do you remember a lot of talking involved in your learning?

11. Discuss how much listening played a role in your learning.

12. What do you remember learning?

13. What words could characterize your experience?

14. What were some valuable characteristics of your schooling in the one-room school? Do you think these could be used in modern education?

15. What was your career in the world of work?

16. Do you read and/or write much now? In your work? In your personal life?

17. What are some memories of relationships with other students in your one-room school?

Appendix III
Instructions for Respondents' Timed Writings

Just a note about what I'm asking you to do:

First, let me thank you for giving me your time and help in the work that I'm trying to do. I appreciate and value all that you say about your experience in the one-room schools of Buckingham County.

I've brought you this notebook so that you can use it to do a series of short writings focusing on the questions you'll find at the top of several pages in it. Don't try to do more than two or three questions in a day over the course of the next two weeks. One question at a time is all I ask you to think about.

I think the best way to begin this is to do short timed writings. Time yourself for ten minutes from the time you start writing to the time you stop. You'll find ten minutes to be satisfying if you keep writing continuously. Don't bother about the writing being correct. Don't stop writing to worry about whether your sentences are complete or your words are spelled right. Just keep putting the words that come into your head about the question down on the paper. When you can't think of anything else, write "I'm stuck" or "I can't think of anything else." Keep on writing words like that, and eventually you will think of something else. Just keep that pen or pencil moving for the allotted time.

This kind of writing works to bring to mind things you had forgotten or didn't think were related. I know it does. I use it all the time. Feel free to go back and add what you want to your writing about each question after your first writing on it. Don't erase anything, though. Sometimes it is necessary to make what you wrote the first time clearer. If you write only on fronts of the pages the first time, then you can go back and write whatever you may want to add or make clearer.

When I return to pick up the book, we'll talk for a bit about this whole experience. I will return for the book in two weeks unless you call me earlier to say you are finished. When I write my paper, I'll be looking at all the material I get from all the people who have been kind enough to do this for me and taking from it information which seems to me important. I will not quote you directly without your approval. No one else will see the material without your consent. I hope you will be interested in looking at my paper when it is finished.

Again, thank you for your kind co-operation and your time. I appreciate your willingness to share a bit of your life experience with me.

Appendix III

Respondent's Release Form

I, _____, have examined the text from my interview with
Susan R. Mondschein which she has used in her dissertation in partial fulfillment of the
degree of Doctor of Education at the Curry School of Education at the University of
Virginia. I approve her use, her provided context, and her interpretations of text from my
interview.

_____Signature _____Date

Bibliography

Adams, Barbara, and Betty Bevans. *Shelby County, Ohio One-Room Schools*. Sidney, OH: Shelby County Genealogical Society, 1993.

Adams, Barbara, and Betty Bevans. *Shelby County, Ohio One-Room Schools. Book 2*. Sidney, OH: Shelby County Genealogical Society, 1996.

Alkire, Phil. "One-Room School—Still Alive and Well in South Dakota." *Small School Forum* 3, no. 3 (1982): 16-18.

Anderson, Norman. "I Remember Springdale School." *Rural Education* 2 (1987): 1-3.

Banks, Smith Callaway, and Daniel Edenfield. *Bulloch County One-Room Schools: A Walk through Time*. Statesboro, Ga: Auspices, Bulloch County Historical Society, 2001.

Barker, Bruce. "Teachers in the Nation's Surviving One-Room Schools." *Contemporary Education* 3 (1986a): 148-50.

Barker, Bruce O. "Where Two or Three Are Gathered Together: A Profile of One-Teacher Schools." *Texas Tech Journal of Education* 1 (1986b): 35-40.

Barker, Bruce, et al. "One-Teacher Schools in America Today." Paper presented at the 76th Annual Conference of the Rural Education Association, Olympia, WA., October 1984.

Barker, Bruce, and Ivan Muse. "One-Room Schools of Nebraska, Montana, South Dakota, California, and Wyoming." *Research in Rural Education* 3 (1986): 127-30.

Barthell, Robert J. "Northwestern Wyoming's Country Schools." In *Country School Legacy: Humanities on the Frontier*. Silt, CO: Mountain Plains Library Association, 1981.

Barthell, Robert J. "Wyoming's Country Schools: Comprehensive Report." In *Country School Legacy: Humanities on the Frontier*. Silt, CO: Mountain Plains Library Association, 1981.

Berg, Paul. *Increasing the Efficiency of the One-Room School*. Cold Bay, AK: Aleutian Region School District, 1977. (ERIC Document Reproduction Service No. 270 250).

Bertani, Katharine. *A Program for Art in Schools*. Brisbane, Australia: Priority Country Area Program Office Report No. 3, 1986.

Berthoff, Ann. "The Teacher as Researcher." In *Reclaiming the Classroom: Teacher Research as an Agency for Change*, edited by Dixie Goswami and Peter R. Stillman. Portsmouth, NH: Heinemann-Boynton-Cook, 1987.

Birkinshaw, Scott B. "The Legacy of Utah's Country Schools." In *Country School Legacy: Humanities on the Frontier.* Silt, CO: Mountain Plains Library Association, 1981.

Blackwood, Lance. *More Like a School Family Than Just a Teacher and His/her Students. Is a One-Teacher School For You?* Anchorage, AK: L.C.'s Manner Publications, 1982.

Bloom, Allen. *The Closing of the American Mind: How Higher Education Has Failed Democracy and Impoverished the Souls of Today's Students.* New York: Simon and Schuster, 1987.

Blue, Edwin G. "Apples Passed Over: A Study of Certain Environmental Aspects of the One-Room School." PhD diss., Indiana University, 1975.

Bowen, Genevieve May. *Living and Learning in a Rural School.* New York: Macmillan and Co, 1946.

Boyken, J. Clarine J. *Echoes of Spring Valley.* Titonka, IA: Author, 1978.

Brinkman, Grover. "This One-Room School Is Fighting to Live and Winning." *American School Board Journal* 165 (1978): 38-39.

Brown, Phillip L. "The Young Citizens' League: Its Growth and Development in South Dakota to 1930." In *Country School Legacy: Humanities on the Frontier.* Silt, CO: Mountain Plains Library Association, 1981.

Burton, Eva Potts, and Virginia R. Wakefield. *Wyoming Legacy: Little Powder River School, 1923-1938.* Cheyenne, Wyo: Anticipation Press, 2000..

Bush, Gail Kiley, and Ruth Lamb. *Rural School Days: The One-Room Schools of Blue Springs, Missouri.* Independence, Mo: Blue and Grey Book Shoppe, 1999.

Casteel, Hazel H., Ernest J. Nesius, and Joseph L. Fasching. *One-Room Schools in Monongalia County, West Virginia.* Morgantown, W. Va: Monongalia Historical Society, 1997..

Coles County Regional Planning Commission, United States, and Illinois Historic Preservation Agency. *Coles County One-Room Schools, 1828-1986.* [Illinois]: The Commission, 1986.

Cousins, Jack. *Rural School Communities in Colorado.* 1983. (ERIC Document Reproduction Service No. ED 239 800).

Covert, Timon. *Educational Achievements of One-Teacher and Larger Rural Schools.* (DHEW Bulletin No. 15). Washington, D.C.: Office of Education 28.

Dewalt, Mark. "One-Room Schools in the United States." Paper presented at the meeting of the Eastern Educational Research Association, Savannah, GA., February 24, 1989.

Dewalt, Mark, and Bonnie Troxell. "Case Study of an Old-Order Mennonite One-Room School." Paper presented at the annual meeting of the American Educational Research Association, New Orleans, LA, April 5-9, 1988.

Dewey, John. "The Child and the Curriculum." In *John Dewey on Education: Selected Writings* edited by Reginald D. Archambault. Chicago: University of Chicago Press, 1964.

Dodds, Joanne L., and Edwin Dodds. "Country School Legacy Report for Colorado." In *Country School Legacy: Humanities on the Frontier.* Silt, CO: Mountain Plains Library Association, 1981.

Dropkin, Ruth, ed. *Recollections of a One-Room Schoolhouse (An Interview with Marian Brooks).* New York: City College Workshop Center for Open Education, 1975.

Dungey, Irma, and Phyllis Habeck. *One Room Rural Schools of Crook County.* [S.l.]: R. and K. Mallak, 1985.

Ediger, Marlow. *Old-Order Amish, Culture, and the Language Arts*, 1983. (ERIC Document Reproduction Service No. ED 241 193).

Ediger, Marlow. *Old-Order Amish and the Philosophy of Education*, 1985. (ERIC Document Reproduction Service No. ED 261 837).

Egerton, John. "One-Teacher Schools Are Still Around." *The Education Digest* (January, 1967): 12-14.

Eidson, Deborah Klinker. *Allen County, Indiana, One-Room School Records, 1858-1958*. Monroeville, Ind: D. Eidson, 2009.

Embry, Jessie L. "Schoolmarms of Utah: Separate and Unequal." In *Country School Legacy: Humanities on the Frontier*. Silt, CO: Mountain Plains Library Association, 1981.

Embry, Jessie L. "Utah's Country Schools since 1896." In *Country School Legacy: Humanities on the Frontier*. Silt, CO: Mountain Plains Library Association, 1981.

Fader, Daniel, James Duggins, Tom Finn, and Elton McNeil. *The New Hooked on Books*. New York, NY: Berkley Books, 1976.

Fogarty, M.F. *A Multiple Progress Plan for the Small School?* Kelvin Grove, Australia: North Brisbane College, 1982.

Freire, Paulo. Translated by Myra Bergman Ramos. *Pedagogy of the Oppressed*. New York: Continuum Books, 1985.

Freire, Paulo, and Donaldo Macedo. *Literacy: Reading the Word and the World*. South Hadley, MA: Bergin and Garvey, 1987.

Fuller, Wayne. *The Old Country School: The Story of Rural Education in the Middle West*. Chicago: University of Chicago Press, 1982.

Gardener, Clark E. "A Survey of Rural Schools in Montana." *Principal* 65, no. 1 (1984): 6-12.

Glasser, William. *Control Theory in the Classroom*. New York, NY: Harper and Row, 1986.

Glenn, Matthew W. "Curriculum Planning in a Queensland One-Teacher School." *Forum for the Discussion of New Trends in Education*, 23, no. 1 (1980): 25-26.

Gray, Pearl Spears. "African-American Folkloric Form and Function in Segregated One-Room Schools." PhD diss., Oregon State University, 1985.

Grundy, Ernest. "The Country School in Literature." In *Country School Legacy: Humanities on the Frontier*. Silt, CO: Mountain Plains Library Association, 1981.

Gulliford, Andrew. *America's Country Schools*. Washington, D.C.: Preservation Press, 1984.

Gulliford, Andrew. "Documenting America's Country Schools." Paper presented at the History of Agricultural Education Symposium, Athens, GA., June 1985a.

Gulliford, Andrew. "The One-Room School Lives!" *Principal* 65, no. 1 (1985b): 6-12.

Gulliford, Andrew, et al. "Work and Leisure in Country Schools in Wyoming." In *Country School Legacy: Humanities on the Frontier*. Silt, CO: Mountain Plains Library Association, 1981.

Guibert, Rita. *Seven Voices: Latin American Poets Talk to Rita Guibert*. New York: Alfred A. Knopf, 1973.

Haack, Paul, et al. "Architectural Aspects of Kansas Country Schools." In *Country School Legacy: Humanities on the Frontier*. Silt, CO: Mountain Plains Library Association, 1981.

Haughey, Margaret, and Peter Murphy. "Preparing Student Teachers for Appointments in Rural Schools." Paper presented to Associated Teacher Education of Europe, Denmark, September 1983.

Hause, Richard G. "I Remember Independence School. *Small School Forum* 4, no. 3 (1983): 3-5.

Heatwole, Cornelius J. *A History of Education in Virginia.* New York: Macmillan and Co, 1916.

Helton, J. Larry. *Southwestern Ohio Early Schools, Mills, Covered Bridges, Depots, Round Barns.* [Ohio]: Society for the Preservation of Ohio One Room Schools, 1993.

Helton, J. Larry. *Jefferson Twp. Schools: a Brief History, 1809-1996.* Middletown, Ohio: J.L. Helton, Society for the Preservation of Ohio One Room Schools, 1996.

Hendricks, Ruth. "Current Practices in the Supervision of One-Room Schools in West Virginia." Master's thesis, American University, 1961.

Hepler, Linda McGhee. 1993. *Good Ol' Golden School Days: Memories of Barbour County, West Virginia One-Room Schools.* [West Virginia?]: L.M. Hepler.

Herndon, James. *The Way It Spozed to Be.* New York: Simon and Schuster, 1968.

Hirsch, E.D., Jr. *Cultural Literacy: What Every American Needs to Know.* New York: Houghton-Mifflin, 1987.

Hough, Jane. 1900. *Diary of a One-Room School.* S.l: s.n.

Howard, Wendell. "Progessing Education." *Phi Delta Kappan* 66, no. 10 (1985): 707-10.

Hughes, Alice M., and Nancy Hughes Dulmage. 2004. *Dear Old Golden Rule Days: A History of the One-Room Schools of Wolford Township.* [Ontario?]: A. M. Hughes and N. H. Dulmage.

Hughes, Warren. *The One-Teacher School: A Disappearing Institution.* Washington, D.C.: Center for Education Statistics, (Report No. 70), 1986.

Jenness, Mary. 1969. *Twelve Negro Americans.* Freeport, N.Y.: Books for Libraries Press.

Johnson, Charlie H., Jr. "Some Historical Background to the Country School Legacy Project: Frontier and Rural Schools in Colorado, 1859-1950." In *Country School Legacy: Humanities on the Frontier.* Silt, CO: Mountain Plains Library Association, 1981.

Johnson, Marilyn Kay, et al. *The Big Job in the Small Schools; or In a One-Teacher School, Can you Call it Mainstreaming?* (ERIC Document Reproduction Service No. 245 845), 1983.

Judge, Sara E. "Eastern and Central Kansas Country Schools." In *Country School Legacy: Humanities on the Frontier.* Silt, CO: Mountain Plains Library Association, 1981.

Kindley, Mark. "Little Schools on the Prairie Still Teach a Big Lesson." *Smithsonian*, 16 no. 7, (1985): 118-31.

Kleinfeld, Judith, and G. Williamson McDiarmid. *Effective Schooling in Rural Alaska: Information for the Rural Effective Schools Project.* Fairbanks, AK: Alaska University Institute of Social, Economic and Government Research, 1983.

Kortright, Agnes R. 1996. *One and Two Room Schoolhouses of the Tri-Valley School District.* S.l: s.n.].

Kozol, Johnathan. *Death at an Early Age: The Destruction of the Hearts and Minds of Negro Children in the Boston Public Schools.* Boston: Houghton-Mifflin, 1967.

Kozol, Johnathan. *Illiterate America.* Garden City, NJ: Anchor Press/Doubleday, 1985.

Knight, Edgar W. *Public Education in the South.* New York: Ginn, 1922.

Kurz, Joanne. "Classroom Spaces: A Descriptive Case Study of a One-Room School in Alaska." PhD diss., University of Oregon, 1983.

Kurtz, Vera Gerken. "My First Year at School, 1895." *Learning* 4, no. 6 (1976): 22-27.

Lau, Donald, and Shirley Sager. 2006. *A History of the One-Room Schoolhouses in the Town of Holland, Sheboygan County, Wisconsin.* [Sheboygan County, Wis.]: Sheboygan County Historical Research Center.

Lincoln, Yvonna S., and Egon G. Guba. *Naturalistic Inquiry.* Beverly Hills, CA: Sage Publications, 1985.

Link, William A. *A Hard Country and a Lonely Place: Schooling, Society, and Reform in Rural Virginia, 1870-1920.* Chapel Hill, NC: University of North Carolina Press, 1986.

Link, William A. "Public Schools and Social Change, 1870-1920." PhD diss. The University of Virginia, 1981.

Link, William A. "Rough Times: Rural Education in Late-nineteenth Century Virginia. *Virginia Cavalcade* (Summer, 1987a): 16-27.

Link, William A. "Rough Times: Rural Education in Late-nineteenth Century Virginia." *Virginia Cavalcade* (Autumn 1987): 86-95.

Masson-Douglas, Jeanne Una. "Learning Environments of Small Rural Schools: A Profile of Selected One-Room Schools in Rural Communities of New England." PhD diss., University of Massachusetts, 1982.

Miller, Bruce A. *Teacher Preparation for Rural Schools.* Portland, OR: Northwest Regional Educational Laboratory, 1988.

Monahan, A.C. *The Status of Rural Education in the United States.* Washington, DC: U.S. Bureau of Education. (Bulletin No. 8.), 1913.

Mountain Plains Library Association. "Instructions to Staff Members prior to Beginning Research." In *Country School Legacy: Humanities on the Frontier.* Silt, CO: Mountain Plains Library Association, 1981.

Muse, Ivan, et al., "A Study of the Performance of Students from Small Country Elementary Schools When They Attend High School." Paper presented at the National Rural Education Conference, Cedar Rapids, IA., October 1985.

Muse, Ivan, et al., *The One-Teacher School in the 1980's.* Fort Collins, CO: National Rural Education Association, 1987.

National Committee on Excellence in Education. *A Nation at Risk: The Imperative for Educational Reform.* Washington, DC: U.S. Government, 1983.

Nash, R., et al., "The One-Teacher School." *British Journal of Educational Studies* 24, no. 1 (1976): 12-32.

New Marion Memories Committee. *New Marion Memories: A History of Shelby Township and New Marion School.* Utica, Ky: McDowell Publications, 1994.

Odell, Ruth Winters, and Mary Frances Reed. *One Room Country Schools in Jackson County, Ohio: Records Collected and Preserved by Mary F. Reed.* S.l: s.n.], 1987.

One-Teacher Schools in the States of the Old Confederacy. Nashville, TN: Southern Education Reporting Service, 1966.

Pait, Gladysteen Hester. *I Remember Bladen County's One Room Schools: School Days.* Bladenboro, NC: Bladenboro Visual Arts Council, 1900.

Pictou County Genealogy & Heritage Society. *Slates to Computers: A History of the One Room School Houses That Gave Way to Make West Pictou Consolidated.* [Pictou, N.S.]: [Pictou County Genealogy & Heritage Society], 2000..

Pitt County Oral History Project. *A Team of Mules and a One-Room School: Memories of Pitt County.* Greenville, N.C.: Pitt County Community Schools, 1981.

Rice, Russ. "The Last Class at Daniel's Creek." *Appalachia* 20, no. 2 (1987): 16-22.

Riske, Milton. "Southeastern Wyoming's Country Schools." In *Country School Legacy: Humanities on the Frontier.* Silt, CO: Mountain Plains Library Association, 1981.

Rowley, Monna Milton. 2002. *Remembering the One-Room Schoolhouse: With Pre-history of Wells Corner School*. [Illinois]: Will County Historical Society.

Sands, Lu. "Jesse Stuart: Lessons from the Kentucky Hills." *Journal of Rural and Small Schools* 1, no. 1 (1986): 13-14.

Scheel, Eugene M., and K. Edward Lay. *"-- to the Colored People of Waterford and Vicinity": a Study of the Architecture and History of Their One-Room School, Waterford, Loudoun County, Virginia*. Studies in vernacular Architecture, SVA-48. Charlottesville, Va: University of Virginia, School of Architecture, 1979.

The Schools of the Glens: A History of the One-Room Schools of Lochiel and Northeast Kenyon of Glengarry County and the Fringes of Prescott County by the Teachers and Students of Those Schools. Vankleek, Ont: L.A. Sproule Pub, 1992.

Schultz, Karla A. *A Room of One's Own : Self-chosen Schools for African-American Students in American Public Schools ; A Thesis*. Boston: University of Massachusetts at Boston, 1993.

Schwarz, Peter, and John Ogilvie. *The Emergent Paradigm: Changing Patterns of Thought and Belief*. Menlo Park, CA: SRI International, 1979.

Scott County Missouri Historical & Genealogy Society. 2009. *One-Room Schools of Scott County, Mo*. [Benton, Mo.]: Scott County Missouri Historical Society.

Scott, Michael. *La Prairie Country Schools: Brief History of the One-Room Schools of LaPrairie Township, Rock County, Wisconsin*. Rock County, Wis: Rock County Historical Society, 1982.

Scott, Robert J. *Teaching and Learning in Remote Schools: A Dilemma beyond Rural Education*. Rosslyn, VA: InterAmerica Research Associates, 1984.

Sharp County Historical Society. *A History of the One-Room Schools of Sharp County: Country School Memories*. Batesville, Ark: Riverside Graphics, 1986.

Slavin, Robert. *Co-operative Learning*. Washington, D.C.: National Education Association, 1982.

Smith, Daniel Tysen. "Appalachia's Last One-Room School: A Case Study (Kentucky)." PhD diss., University of Kentucky, 1988.

Smith, Lester J., Ward F. Rohm, and Marjorie J. Davis. *100+ years of One-Room Schools in Springfield Township, Oakland County, Michigan*. Springfield Twp., MI?: Marjorie J. Davis?, 2007.

Smith, Mary Lee, and Gene V. Glass. *Research and Evaluation in Education and the Social Sciences*. Englewood Cliffs, NJ: Prentice-Hall Inc, 1987.

Spencer, John Corson. "Some Problems in the Organization and Programs of Small High Schools in Virginia." Master's thesis, Duke University, Durham, 1937.

Sprigle, Ray. *In the Land of Jim Crow*. New York: Simon and Schuster, 2007.

Stanton, Harry. "The British Way: Vertical Grouping." *Teacher* 90, no. 5 (1973): 106-8.

Stuart, Jesse. *To Teach, To Love*. New York: World Publishing, 1970.

Stuart, Jesse. *The Thread That Runs So True*. New York: Scribner's, 1949.

Stuttgen, Joanne Raetz. *One-Room and Two-Room Country Schoolhouses of Morgan County, Indiana: An Architectural History*. Indiana?: s.n., 1994.

Sullivan, Joan. *One Room Rural Schools in the Valley of the Bears: "La Cañada de los Osos."* Los Osos, CA: The Bay News, 2002.

Swaim, Jean Nipps. *The Era of the One-Room Rural School in Cedar County, Missouri*. Springfield, Mo: Barnabas Pub. Services, 1999.

Swanson, Leslie. *Rural One-Room Schools of Mid-America*. Moline, IL: Author, 1984.

Terkel, Studs. *American Dreams: Lost and Found*. New York: Pantheon Books, 1980.

Terkel, Studs. *Hard Times: An Oral History of America in the Depression*. New York: Pantheon Books, 1966.

Tierney, Michael T. "Bread on the Water: Education in an Isolated Mountain Community." *Human Services in the Rural Environment* 8, no. 3 (1983): 3-11.

Tucker, Gregory. *Remembering Rutherford.* Charleston, SC: History Press, 2010.

Virginia Department of Education. *Fall Membership Records, 1988-89.* Richmond, VA: Virginia Department of Education, 1989.

Washington State Superintendent of Public Instruction. *One-Room Schools in Washington State.* Olympia, WA: Washington Department of Education, 1981.

White, Charles W. *The Hidden and the Forgotten: Contributions of Buckingham Blacks to American History.* Marceline, MO: Walsworth Press, 1985.

Williams, Tony L. "A Salute to the West Virginia One-Room Schools." *Journal of Rural and Small Schools* 1, no. 2 (1986): 29-32.

Wolff, Priscilla B., and C. Gordon Porter. *Annie, Annie Over: A Year in a One-Room School.* Barker (N.Y.): Town of Somerset Historical Society, 1992.

Zimmerman, Lori J. *A Glimpse at the Past.* Manheim, PA: Manheim Central School District, 1992.

Relevant Web Sources

"Civil Rights." http://www.vahistorical.org/civilrights/pec.html.

Clerk of the House of Representatives, "Final vote results for roll-call 145." May 23, 2001. http://clerk.house .gov/evs/2001/roll145.xml.

Country School Association. "Modern One-Room School." http://www .countryschoolassociation.org/ModernOneRoomSchool.pdf.

Inskeep, Steve. "Former 'No Child Left Behind' Advocate Turns Critic." http://www.npr .org/templates/story/story.php?storyId=124209100&ps=cprs.

Library of Congress. "Bill Summary & Status 107th Congress (2001 - 2002) H.R.1 CRS Summary." http:// thomas .loc .gov/ cgi-bin/ bdquery/ z?d107 :HR00001: @@@D&summ2=0&.

Library of Congress, "To close the achievement gap with accountability, flexibility, and choice, so that no child is left behind." http://www.loc.gov/index.html.

"Looping in Education: Time to Make It a Fundamental Practice." www.openeducation .net/.../looping-in-education-time-to-make-it-a-fundamental-practice/.

Nichols, Sandra. "The Federal Government's No Child Left Behind Act (NCLB — dubbed 'nicklebee')." *When NCLB Standards Meet Reality*, (April 26, 2003), http://web .archive .org/ web/ 20070806232831/ www .tellingthetruth .com/ education_matters/ESSAYS_03/sandra_0403.html.

North Central Regional Educational Laboratory Learning Point Associates. *Looping.* http://www.ncrel.org/sdrs/areas/issues/methods/instrctn/in5lk10.htm.

"Senate Roll Call Vote." U.S. Department of Education. "Press Releases," 2006-02-06. http://www.npr.org/templates/story/story.php?storyId=124209100&ps=cprs.

U.S. Department of Education Institute of Education Sciences. "National Assessment of Adult Literacy (NAAL): A nationally representative and continuing assessment of English language and literary skills of American Adults." http://nces.ed.gov/NAAL/ kf_demographics.asp.

U.S. Department of Education. "Fiscal Year 2007 Budget Request Advances NCLB Implementation and Pinpoints Competitiveness" 2006-02-06. http://www2.ed.gov/ news/pressreleases/2006/02/02062006.html.

U.S. Senate Roll Call Votes 107th Congress - 1st Session. <u>H.R. 1</u> (No Child Left Behind
    Act of 2001) http:// www .senate .gov/ legislative/ LIS/ roll_call_lists/
    roll_call_vote_cfm.cfm?congress=107&session=1&vote=00192.

Wikipedia Encyclopedia, s.v. "No Child Left Behind Act," http://en.wikipedia.org/wiki/
    No_Child_Left_Behind_Act^ .

Index

www.ingramcontent.com/pod-product-compliance
Lightning Source LLC
Chambersburg PA
CBHW030655270326
41929CB00007B/378